THE TRAINING
OF WILD ANIMALS

Frank C. Bostock

THE TRAINING
OF WILD ANIMALS

BY

FRANK CHARLES BOSTOCK

EDITED BY

ELLEN VELVIN, F.Z.S.

AUTHOR OF "RATAPLAN: A ROGUE
ELEPHANT," ETC.

Fredonia Books
Amsterdam, The Netherlands

The Training of Wild Animals

by
Frank Charles Bostock

ISBN: 1-4101-0287-4

Copyright © 2003 by Fredonia Books

Reprinted from the 1911 edition

Fredonia Books
Amsterdam, The Netherlands
http://www.fredoniabooks.com

THIS BOOK IS DEDICATED
TO MY SON
FRANCIS EDWARD BOSTOCK

CONTENTS

LIST OF ILLUSTRATIONS

ix

* From photographs by Hall.

EDITOR'S NOTE

BEFORE editing this book, I took the opportunity offered by Mr. Frank C. Bostock of practically living in one of his animal exhibitions for a few weeks, in order to see things as they were, and not as I had always heard of them.

I was allowed to go in and out at all times and all hours; to enter the training-schools whenever I liked; to go behind the runways and cages,—a special privilege given to the trainers only, as a rule,—and to be a spectator of whatever happened to be going on at the time.

The thing which interested me most, and to which I paid special attention, was that at no time in this exhibition did I once see the slightest act of cruelty in any way. Each one of the trainers and keepers had pride in his own special animals, and I had many proofs of their kindness and consideration to their charges. The sick animals were most carefully looked after and doctored, and in one case of a lion cub having convulsions, I noticed dim eyes in more than one keeper when the poor little animal was convulsed and racked with suffering.

Had I seen the least cruelty or neglect in any way, I need scarcely say nothing would have induced me to edit this book.

ELLEN VELVIN.

NEW YORK CITY,
June 8th, 1903.

PREFACE

THE big and little men and women of the jungle have ever fascinated me. As a child, I used often to romp with cubs attached to the traveling menageries of my parents and grandfather. Most of my boyhood, and virtually all of my youth, was passed in the almost daily companionship of wild animals. At no time have these far-traveled aliens failed to interest me. Indeed, I believe the subject engrosses me more to-day than it ever did. No two members of a species are alike. Their individualities are as clearly marked as are ours of the bigger life. I early learned that certain traits of my animal acquaintances were easily to be likened to qualities of real men and women. Longer acquaintance ripened my knowledge and understanding. Many and many a lion and tiger have I known that were quite as mean and untrustworthy as men. Others I met in plenty who would scorn an unfair advantage. Most of them I found to be fair, considerate, friendly, and genuinely affectionate. In time I learned to understand my fellows of the cages, got as close, perhaps, as it is possible for man to get to mute creatures, and enjoyed the assurance that they understood and appreciated me.

In my earlier years, I did n't, I fear, altogether appreciate the good fortune of this companionship; but later, when maturity and reflection illumined my way, I was duly grateful for these friends, and, from being fond of but some, gradually grew to love all. Recognizing as I did with my broadening life the limitations of their knowledge of us, I learned not to blame the slow or the rebellious.

At about this period of my career as a trainer and exhibitor, it occurred to me that perhaps I was wrong in being the jailer of these friends; that doubtless their original freedom of forest, desert, and jungle was their right,—one that could not be trespassed upon with honesty. The question of whether I was wrong or right bothered me for a long while, and many an ache I had while wrestling with it. I saw these untamed men and women back in their own; saw them crouching at night in hidden fastnesses, awaiting the coming of prey; saw tragedies of the jungle; recalled too frequent ravages of human life, sometimes from hunger and again through sheer lust. I traced to authentic sources long records of these acquaintances of mine found on their own playgrounds dying and dead from hunger and thirst or the shot of the hunter of sport or gain. I thought, in these reflections, of the horse in his first wild state, of the zebra and the elephant; how these had been reclaimed from truculence with benefit to themselves and humanity. I considered, too, the demands of modern education, the obligations of natural historians, the incalculable value of living objects for study. I knew my friends of the jungle suffered no discomforts with me.

My problem then resolved itself to this: Should I recommit my charges back to their own, and cease abetting further captures, or should I continue to guard and cherish my friends, thus saving them and their weaker neighbors from the certain evils of the wilds?

Surely, I reasoned, their better welfare is assured here with me; they never hunger, thirst, suffer violent deaths, nor administer any. Incontestably they show that captivity is not a hardship. Feeling thus, can I conscientiously abandon them, where by continuing I may benefit them and others.

The result of these and like deliberations was a decision to continue the work of my forebears.

The training of my dumb companions is never cruel,—less so, perhaps, when the difference of organization is considered, than the firmness exercised occasionally in the correction of an evilly disposed child. Kindness is the whip used to lead wild animals to obey. Without it none can be made to understand. With confidence, established and maintained by kindness and gentleness, the most savage beast may be transformed into a willing and even eager pupil. Of course, there are limitations to the intelligence of wild animals.

These limitations are pretty clearly established. The pupils are invariably capable of greater understanding and achievement than they are ever called upon to display. It is quite probable that other generations will carry wild-animal training further, but at the stage at which I have stopped I am content. I understand my associates, and know they understand me. I should be sorry to learn that the thoughtful of the public denied to my devotion the instructive and humane incentives that have sustained it.

For some of the matter of the volume, incorporated from an article[1] on wild-animal training, written after an interview with me, I wish to express my thanks to Mr. S. H. Adams.

F. C. B.

---

[1] "The Training of Lions, Tigers, and other Great Cats," by Samuel Hopkins Adams, "McClure's Magazine," September, 1900.

THE TRAINING
OF WILD ANIMALS

THE TRAINING OF
WILD ANIMALS

CHAPTER I

IN WHICH I BECOME "THE BOY TRAINER"—
A LION HUNT IN A SEWER

ALTHOUGH my family was one of animal trainers and exhibitors, my father did not wish me to follow so hazardous a profession, and decided that I should become a clergyman of the Church of England. My early education was carefully looked after, and having completed my preparatory course under private tutors, I finally went to Kelvedon College in Essex, England, where I did well. I was fond of study, had good masters,—who always impressed upon me the fact that " he who would hope to command must learn to obey,"—and gained some honors.

But during one vacation I went home and

saw my father's wild-animal exhibition, and there all the glamour and fascination of the show came upon me. There is no doubt I had inherited my father's instincts. The lion-tamer my father had at that time was the great feature of the show. It struck me, however, that he was extremely cruel, and being very fond of animals myself, this aroused my indignation. I spoke to my father about it rather warmly, but he, evidently thinking it a boy's impetuosity, laughed it off, saying the man was only protecting himself.

That same evening, however, the trainer handled the lion so roughly that, enraged at the injustice and indignities to which he was subjected, the animal suddenly turned upon him, and would certainly have killed him had not prompt assistance been rendered.

Wrought up and excited by the occurrence, I begged my father to let me take his place, but he would not hear of it. The next day I took the law into my own hands, and it was in the lion's cage that my father found me, to his horror, when casually going the rounds of the show. He watched me for a while in fear and trembling, and then said, his voice quivering with anger and fright:

"If ever you get out of there alive, my lad, I 'll give you the biggest thrashing you ever had in your life."

But he did n't. He was so overjoyed at my safety and so proud of my success, that after much persuasion I got him to allow me to take the place of the incapacitated trainer. I was fifteen at this time, and was called "The Boy Trainer." From that time my college days were over, and I knew there could never be any other life for me than that of a trainer and showman.

I have never regretted this step; but I often look back upon my peaceful college days with great pleasure, for they laid the foundation of good principles, self-control, and discipline; and I have always made it my chief endeavor never to allow anything the least vulgar or offensive in my exhibitions.

There is a fascination about wild-animal training which few who have once felt it escape. The constant presence of danger calls for quick judgment and promptness in meeting an emergency. A thrilling experience of mine in Birmingham, England, in 1889, may show the critical situation in which a wild-animal showman is sometimes placed.

A country fair was being held at the time, very similar to the fairs held in America, which bring into the city country people from all parts, most of whom look upon them as events in their lives.

We had a remarkably fine specimen of an African lion at that time; well formed, well grown, with a handsome head and shoulders covered with a fine darkish mane. He had been much admired, and had been referred to by several naturalists as a typical king of beasts for his haughtiness and dignified bearing.

This lion was, however, one of the greatest worries and anxieties I have ever had. He had killed one man, and wounded several attendants, so powerful were his paws, and so quick his movements in reaching out of his cage. He required the most careful watching at all times, and was a very difficult animal to manage, in spite of unlimited time and patience spent on him. Kindness had no effect on him whatever. Special dainties he took with a growl, watching all the time for the least opportunity to grab and tear the giver. To attempt any sort of punishment or discipline with him would have been fatal; he was far too dangerous an animal to risk arousing his wild nature, and the only thing we could do was to keep him perfectly quiet, see that he was not irritated in any way, and was made as comfortable and happy as was possible, with good food, a clean house, and another lion for companionship.

The second lion was removed from the malcontent by an iron partition, as it appeared a little doubtful how he would be received. We intended transferring both lions on the opening day to a much larger cage, where they would have more space and comfort, and also have a much better opportunity of being seen.

The opening day was remarkable for its fine weather; crowds of people were flocking into the city from all parts, and everything promised to be a huge success. We ran one of our big cages on wheels up to the cage containing the two lions, and placing the cages door to door, dropped a lasso over the quiet lion's neck, and by gentle twitches induced him to enter the big cage.

Then we tried the same tactics with the African lion, but with very different results. Time after time he slipped the noose from his great body and tore madly up and down the cage, as though possessed of the strength of twenty lions. We waited a few minutes until he stopped to roar, and then once more slipped the rope over him. With a terrific wrench and twist he got himself free, and with such a wild bound that the cages shook again he sprang into the next cage so suddenly, and with such terrific force as to cause the wagon to move away upon its wheels; and before the attendants could close the door, he sprang over their heads and into the street, where for the time he was as free and untrammeled as when in his native wilds.

To approach him probably meant death, but in spite of this we tried to capture him with ropes and the lasso, but without success. Suddenly he turned back, dashed through the

MR. BOSTOCK AND HIS EIGHT LIONS

lions' tent to the rear of the building, pushed himself through a rift, and made off for the city of Birmingham, which contained at that time over two hundred thousand people.

On his way he came to one of the openings of the many sewers which empty the waste of the city, and down he sprang, looking up at the crowd of people and roaring at the top of his voice. In about twenty minutes nearly every person in Birmingham knew what had happened, and the greatest consternation prevailed everywhere. The fear was intensified by the fact that as the lion made his way through the sewers, he stopped at every manhole he came to, and there sent up a succession of roars that echoed and reverberated until the very earth seemed to be full of weird sounds, driving some of the people nearly wild with terror.

I was at my wits' end. There was the danger of the lion escaping from the sewer at any moment and killing some one, for which I should be responsible, while there was also the greater danger that there would be a riot among the crowd. Something must be done to allay their fears, and quickly. People were beginning to flock toward the menagerie in thousands, with anything but complimentary speeches.

After one of the worst quarters of an hour I ever spent, I gathered as many of my men as could be spared from the show, put a lion into a large shifting-cage, and covering the whole thing with canvas, in order that the lion should not be seen, we set off for the mouth of the sewer, all armed with as many ropes, pitchforks, pistols, etc., as we could carry. On arriving, we placed the cage at the mouth of the sewer, with the door facing it. I knew perfectly well that the lion would much prefer to remain in his cage than to enter the darkness of that evil-smelling sewer, and so it proved.

Then, with three of my attendants, I went three blocks back, lowering ropes down each of the manholes on our way until we pretended we had found the lion, and then I lowered myself into the depths through the third manhole. The next thing was to fire blank cartridges, blow horns, and shout as loudly as possible, and, owing to the peculiar echo, the noise was deafening. One of the attendants had been instructed at a given signal to lift the iron door of the cage up and down quickly, and then suddenly clap the door down with a shout.

Everything went off well. At the sound of the door closing, a shout went up from the crowd:

"They've got him! They've got him! They've got the lion!"

The cage containing the lion was then driven quickly toward the menagerie, with myself and attendants seated on top, followed by an admiring crowd of thousands of people. When we finally reached the front of the exhibition, some of the men in the crowd rushed forward and carried me in victory on their shoulders into the menagerie, while the cage containing the bogus lion was restored to its original place in the menagerie. Over forty thousand people filed into the show, until we were positively obliged to refuse admission to any more.

Meanwhile I was in a perfect bath of cold perspiration, for matters were extremely serious, and I knew not what to do next. The fears of the people were allayed for the time, and a probable riot had been stopped only just in time, but the lion was still in the sewer. He might get out at any moment—might be out even then, for all I knew—or he might roar again and so let his whereabouts be known and my deception, which would cause a greater riot than before.

As soon as possible I placed trusty men with iron bars at the mouth of the sewer; and as, fortunately, the lion stopped his roaring, and contented himself with perambulating up and down the sewer through the narrow miles of tunneling, things were quiet for the time. When everything had been done that was possible I went to bed, but as that was the most anxious night I have ever had, it is scarcely necessary for me to say that sleep was out of the question.

On the afternoon of the following day, the chief of police of Birmingham came to see me, and congratulated me on my marvelous pluck and daring. This made me feel worse than before, and I at once made a clean breast of the whole thing. I shall never forget that man's face when he realized that the lion was still in the sewer: it was a wonderful study for any mind-reader. At first he was inclined to blame me; but when I showed him I had probably stopped a panic, and that my own liabilities in the matter were pretty grave possibilities to face, he sympathized with me, and added that any help he could give me, I might have.

I at once asked for five hundred men of the police force, and also asked that he would instruct the superintendent of sewers to send me the bravest men he could spare, with their top-boots, ladders, ropes, and revolvers with them, so that should the lion appear, any man could do his best to shoot him at sight. We arranged that we should set out at five minutes to twelve, midnight, so that we might avoid any crowd following us, and so spreading the report.

At the appointed time, the police and sewermen turned out, and I have never seen so many murderous weapons at one time in my life. Each man looked like a walking arsenal, but every one of them had been sworn to secrecy, and there was determination and desire for adventure on the face of each one. Among so many, and with so much ammunition, the danger had diminished to a minimum, provided the lion did not get one man at a time cornered in some narrow place.

The police and sewer-men were to be stationed at every manhole in every district in which the lion was believed to be, within a radius of a mile. The empty cage was brought and placed at the mouth of the sewer, the other end of which had been blocked up so that the lion's only means of exit was the open door of the cage.

Then three trusty men and myself, accompanied by my giant boar-hound, Marco, lowered ourselves into the manhole, crawling on our hands and knees, and not knowing at any moment when we should come upon the lion. With such suddenness that we all jumped, Marco gave a sharp bark, followed by a curious throaty growl, and I knew that the faithful creature had found the scent and was giving warning of the enemy's whereabouts.

This boar-hound of mine had been trained

to perform with wild animals and lions, and was a stanch and game fighter. He was not to be cowed by any lion on earth, but if he could only once get a hold, would hang on like grim death. As we went slowly and cautiously along, I suddenly saw two gleaming eyes of greenish-red just beyond, and knew we were face to face with the lion at last.

I at once sent one man back to shout the location of the runaway to the others, and then, dropping on all fours, blowing horns, firing off blank cartridges, and letting off Roman candles,—which spat and fizzed in a most uncanny manner in the tunnel,—we went cautiously forward, hoping to drive the lion to his cage, only two blocks away.

But at this juncture a terrific fight took place between the boar-hound and the lion, and it is needless to say that the danger to all parties under these circumstances in that narrow, dark sewer was extremely great. It was not until the boar-hound had been severely slashed and torn by the lion on his shoulders and hind quarters, and his head badly bitten in several places, that he left his savage antagonist and came to me with a whimper for protection. He had held on until he was at his last gasp, and had let go only just in time to save his life. I sent him back to the men to be taken care of, and then went on with the fight myself.

Taking off my big jack-boots, I put them on my hands and arms, and going up close to the lion, was fortunately able to hit him a stinging blow on the nose with one of them. Fearing that he would split my head open with a blow from one of his huge paws, I told one of my men to place over my head a large iron kettle which we had used to carry cartridges and other things to the sewer. While he was trying to fix this, the kettle tipped and rolled over and went crashing down the sewer, making a noise and racket which echoed and resounded throughout the whole length of the narrow tunnel in the most appalling manner.

The lion, who had resisted everything else in the way of capture, at once turned tail like a veritable coward, and, racing down the sewer at a mad gallop, was soon lost to sight, as though the earth had suddenly swallowed him.

HERMAN WEEDON AND HIS GROUP OF LIONS, TIGER, BROWN, TIBET,
AND SLOTH BEARS, SILESIAN BOARHOUNDS, AND HYENA

We wondered where he could have gone, as he had not had time enough to run far, but following him up, we found him in a sorry plight.

There was an eight-foot fall in the rear of the sewer, and this was evidently his reason for being so reluctant to turn back until frightened by the kettle. We did not know of this, and consequently tumbled headlong into it. We were not hurt, and as the lion was now roaring terrifically, we followed him up and soon found out the cause of his trouble. In the act of falling he had caught his hind legs and quarters in one of the slip-nooses which had been dropped down the manhole to secure him, and was hanging head downward from the manhole.

Other strong ropes were let down immediately, for he would soon have died in that position, and we were fortunate enough to secure his head and fore paws. The cage was then placed at the manhole, and when we had run the ropes through the cage and out over the sidewalk, the men began to haul, and in this unkingly fashion the king of beasts was

2

dragged out of his prison and into his cage once more, where he never again had an opportunity to escape. So I got the lion out of the sewer, as the people of Birmingham supposed I did, only their praise and applause were a little previous. But I hope never to have such another terrible experience.

CHAPTER II

ORIGIN AND HISTORY OF WILD-ANIMAL TRAINING

THE arena has been in use for public spectacles and amusements from the earliest ages, and its popularity has never diminished. The great changes, however, which have taken place have developed it into a civilized, instructive spectacle, instead of a barbarous and cruel performance presented only for the purpose of exciting men's passions.

Lions have always played a prominent part in these public amusements and exhibitions. They were led as trophies in the triumphs of semi-barbarians, and were exhibited and sacrificed by thousands in the Roman amphitheater. Six hundred were provided by Pompey for a single festival. That the lion should always have figured thus in history is but natural. He is the king of beasts, and though there are other wild animals more intelligent in some ways, he always has held, and always will hold, this supremacy over all other brutes.

No wild animals were ever trained by the ancients. It was in turning the power and superiority of man over animals to financial account that the art of training wild animals was first conceived, and it was to further financial gain that it has been advanced step by step since, though the final development of each step has been made by a small number of men who have had an inborn love of daring, and an insatiable desire for the accomplishment of the hazardous.

George Wombwell, from whom I am directly descended, was one of the first men who saw the great possibilities in the training of wild animals, although what actually led to the present advanced stage was the result of chance. Wombwell's traveling show was established in England in 1805, and the first wild-animal show, in which the most ferocious of the large felines were used, was formed three years later.

Trained monkeys and many highly trained

THE TOWERING OF THE KINGS

domestic animals were known in Europe, but never before had lions and tigers been subjugated to daily association with men. At that time a traveling show of the Wombwell type was similar in many respects to the great circuses of to-day, its chief point of similarity being its amalgamation with a menagerie. The importation of Asiatic and African animals was, of course, less frequent and more expensive than now, with the result that the menageries were smaller and less diversified. The greatest care was taken of the animals, chiefly on account of their commercial value, but the proprietors were heavily handicapped by their lack of knowledge respecting animal ways and requirements.

It was a matter of frequent occurrence to take any little sick cubs into the family, and nurse and watch over them as one would a sick child. It was on such an occasion that George Wombwell thought of training wild animals as a good business speculation. He had just received two young lions from Africa, and on their arrival they were found to be in an extremely weak condition from bad feeding, neglect of cleanliness, and violent seasickness. It was clear that unless the greatest care and attention were given to them they would very soon die. Wombwell put one man to attend only to these cubs, watching over them night and day, and nursing them with all possible care.

The man who lived with these young lions, ministering to their necessities and comforts, was in daily association with his charges for several weeks, and in that time acquired a familiarity which lessened his fear of them. He fed them daily from his own hands, kept them warm and clean, bedded them with fresh, dry straw morning and evening, dressed, and finally cured the sores which filth and neglect had caused on their sides and limbs, and by the time they were once more in good condition he had developed a strong affection for them.

When he had to leave the lions altogether, he seemed to feel the separation very much, and the idea suggested itself to Wombwell that not only would the exhibition of two lions and a man in the same cage be a distinct novelty, but it would be a splendid financial speculation. There appeared to be very little, if any, danger, now that the three had grown accustomed to one another, so that when the man begged that the association should not be broken, Wombwell told him of his idea, to which he readily consented. In a few days he announced to the provincial public that he would exhibit a " lion-tamer," and thousands came from near and far to witness this wonderful sight. Such was the beginning.

That was less than a hundred years ago. Then two sick cubs with a quiet man sitting between them aroused the curiosity of all England, while now a man goes into the arena with twenty-seven full-grown male lions and makes them perform at the same time!

From that first incident, the advance in animal training for exhibition purposes has been steady. Many things have been done which no one ever believed could be done; many valuable facts and characteristics about wild animals discovered which would, in all probability, never have been known to science otherwise; and a great many lessons learned as to the wonderful power of man over all the animal creation, if exercised in the proper manner.

The advance was much slower at the start than it is now, when every year sees as great improvement in animal training as ten years did a century ago. It was five years before George Wombwell realized that it was possible for almost any animal to be trained and handled if he could only find the right man to do the handling. But that was then, and is now, a matter of the greatest difficulty.

The progress during the first three quarters of the last century was very slow. There were various performances in which a man or a woman entered the arena with wild animals and put them through very elementary drills; but it was within the last twenty years only that the involved groups and elaborate tricks of the present day have been suggested and produced.

Many things were not known formerly respecting the control of animals, which now form the very first essentials for all trainers, and accidents were more frequent and more dangerous. One of Wombwell's most famous trainers was Ellen Bright, a girl who achieved a great reputation. Unfortunately, owing to some slight carelessness on her part, she was killed by a tiger in 1880, when only seventeen years old. Had she only realized more fully the need of patience and firmness with wild animals, there is no doubt whatever that the accident which caused her death would not have taken place.

When it is considered how many trainers there now are, with how many animals they perform at one time, what difficulties they have to face, not only with such numbers, but with such diverse creatures naturally so antagonistic to one another, as in the case of the mixed groups, and how comparatively few accidents happen, it can be readily understood how far this science has progressed.

Perhaps of all the types of animal training these mixed groups are the most wonderful. Lions and tigers instinctively hate each other, and in their native state look with contempt on jackals and hyenas. Were a lion and a tiger to meet in the jungle, it would mean a fight to the death. If two or more male lions meet in their native haunts, a fierce fight is the natural sequence, until only one is left to bear witness by his scars and tears of the terrible battle which has been fought. Should a jackal or a hyena see the king of beasts, he skulks around until his majesty has finished his meal, and then sneaks forward to take the leavings.

And yet, in these mixed groups, lions, tigers, hyenas, sloth-bears, polar bears, and Tibet bears are all together in the same arena; one sits quietly on his pedestal while another goes through his act; the lion has to associate with the hyena; and in some cases two animals, naturally antagonistic to each other, and coming from far corners of the globe, perform together without even showing that they object, and have been subjected to this gross indignity by the superiority of man.

It took Herman Weedon years of patient and painstaking toil and trouble to bring his group to its present state of perfection. The hardest task of all is to accustom animals of one kind to tolerate the presence of animals of another kind. There is always the danger of a fight, which between two wild animals generally ends in the death of one or the other, and the trainer has to consider the interests of his employer as well as the great risk to his own life.

In arranging a mixed group, each animal has to be studied carefully; his idiosyncrasies must be humored, his characteristics must be known and ever borne in mind; the animosity between the wild beasts must be taken into careful consideration, and the methods of teaching must vary with each animal according to its special traits. It means years of patient effort, because it is practically training animal nature against its instincts, and the final result of amity, or assumed amity, between such antagonistic forces is for this reason one of the greatest proofs of the extent of man's power over wild animals.

CHAPTER III

HOUSEKEEPING FOR WILD ANIMALS

THERE are three essentials in the care and
feeding of wild animals—good food,
cleanliness, and exercise. Food and cleanliness come first, but exercise is nearly as important, and this is one of the main reasons
why animals in traveling shows are so much
healthier and stronger than those kept in zo-
ological parks. In the parks they get food
and cleanliness, but little exercise; for wild
animals are proverbially lazy, and, unless
compelled by hunger or force of circumstances, will not exert themselves in the least,
preferring to lie about and sleep rather than
even to walk round their cages.

With trained animals especially, the trainers make it one of their chief objects to give
their animals exercise; first, to keep them in

"THE THREE GRACES"

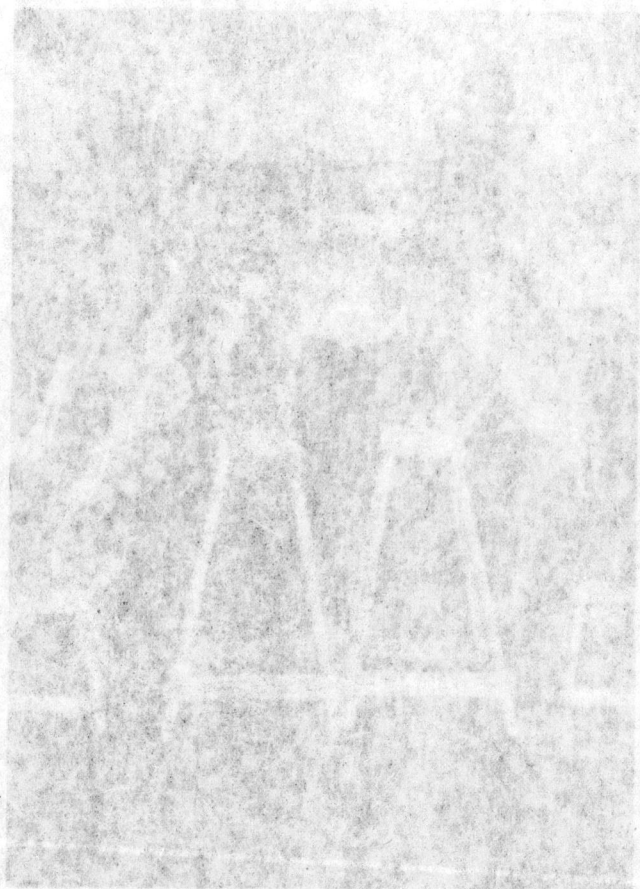

good condition, and, secondly, to make them more alert and active. Captain Bonavita, a well-known trainer, makes it a rule to take out all his lions, whether performing that week or not, and exercise them up and down the passages, the runways behind the cages, or in the arena.

In doing this there are difficulties. All wild animals, especially lions, dislike movement. True, they pace up and down their cages, but this is only when waiting for food, or because they have discovered a stranger in the building and resent it. This pacing is not exercise enough. Think of the miles a lion has to race in his wild state in search of food!

But in captivity there is no inducement to take any exercise at all. He is fed well and regularly, for his commercial value is considerable, and he is well worth taking care of. He knows that he will get his food in some way or other, and so the most he does in the matter is to pace restlessly up and down his small cage and exercise his lungs by roaring occasionally.

Having to go through two performances

a day compels the animal to take a certain amount of regular exercise, which he always resents, but which improves his health and condition. This is the reason that trained animals have such good sleek coats,—a true test of the condition of an animal,—well-grown, thick manes, and clean mouths, feet, and eyes.

There can be no doubt whatever that all wild animals enjoy a change of air and scene. Watch a lion or a tiger when anything strange or unusual takes place. He will rise up and do his best to investigate, and, failing in this, he walks about and roars at the top of his voice. And although this is a little trying to the nerves of some of his hearers, he is all the better for it in many ways.

It has been noticed by many animal owners and trainers, and I have invariably noticed it myself, that the animals grow listless and indifferent after being in one place for a long time; but as soon as they begin to travel, they rouse themselves and take an interest in all that is going on. Very few animals roar or make any sound when traveling, but they are, nevertheless, always on the *qui vive* to know what is happening, and evidently take a great interest in it all. The very movement of the wagons and trains, although occasionally upsetting them for a short time, proves beneficial in stirring up their livers, which often grow torpid from the sedentary life.

Many have the idea that wild animals are very robust, but this is a great mistake. Instead of being in strong and rude health, they are subject to all kinds of ailments, and in many cases have to be looked after as carefully as an infant. Lions are subject to colds and coughs, and to very serious tuberculosis, which often ends fatally in less than eight months, its course being far more rapid with them than with men.

Another trouble with lions is that they are much afflicted with rheumatism, and unless kept in a dry and warm place, get so crippled in the joints that they not only become valueless for show purposes, but very often have to be killed in order to put them out of their misery—a serious loss when a lion has cost over a thousand dollars and has increased his value by becoming a good performer.

Lionesses, too, are subject to a large number of complaints, and even when fairly healthy and strong require unceasing attention. It is a very critical time when a lioness is about to have cubs. The lioness is invariably more restless and much quicker in movement than the lion, but when expecting to become a mother her restlessness is terrible, and her excitement, if allowed to get the least bit beyond her control, very frequently results in her not only killing all her little ones, but actually eating them. And when this has once happened, it is a rare thing ever to make a good mother of her, for she will do it again and again, not through dislike or fear of her offspring, but simply because she is restless and unnerved, and does not seem to know what she is doing in her distress.

Of course, in addition to ordinary complaints, there are other things which affect the health of wild animals. In a free fight among wild beasts, such as happened at one time with Captain Bonavita's lions, the animals received serious injuries. It takes very little to start lions fighting; it is their nature to fight one

"DENVER" AND "CÆSAR"

another, and it is only by training and the wonderful power which Captain Bonavita holds over his animals, that this large number of wild beasts is made to sit calmly round on pedestals and not even touch one another.

In this case Captain Bonavita had turned his twenty-seven lions out into the runway behind the cages in preparation for the performance, when Denver, one of the biggest and fiercest Nubian lions, suddenly started a fight with another lion. In a very few minutes the whole twenty-seven lions were fighting madly in the narrow passageway, with one man among them, for whom at that moment they had nothing but supreme contempt.

Captain Bonavita did his best to separate the animals, and took some desperate chances while doing so, for the lions were only too ready for something to fight; but it was all useless. He shouted orders to them, called them by name, fired blank cartridges, and when he had exhausted his voice, cartridges, and strength, could only take refuge behind one narrow board, into which he had luckily had a handle put only the day before, and do his best to defend himself.

3

This board was not wide enough to cover him, and he had to guard himself carefully, as several lions were trying to get at him through the little space which was left at one side. All he could do was to shift the board constantly, but among so many it was small wonder that at last one of the lions got one huge paw in, and tore a large piece of the trainer's coat and flesh off his chest. By great efforts, however, Bonavita managed to get out alive.

In this terrific fight several of the lions were seriously injured, for the fight lasted over an hour, and it took nearly another hour to get all the animals back into their cages again. One or two were badly bitten and torn, and it was necessary that some sewing and patching should be done. With great caution, ropes were dropped round the neck and legs of each of the injured animals, and in this way they were drawn close to the bars, and the necessary stitches and repairs were accomplished with much difficulty. This is one of the most dangerous things to do to a wild animal, for, in spite of being tied, he is always on the lookout, and can give a bite which would stop the operator forever. But in this case all was got through safely, and the lions eventually recovered.

Animals are always roped in this way when anything is wrong with their teeth, claws, or limbs. It is the only way in which they can be handled at all. As for the notion that many people have that some of the animals are drugged, I need scarcely say that it is absurd. Animals cannot be drugged in that way. To drug wild animals might mean some very serious losses, not to mention the fact that the ultimate effect of the drugs would greatly depreciate their commercial value.

And while speaking of this peculiar delusion of the public, I might, perhaps, also be allowed to mention the mistaken idea that so many have, that cruelty is practised to a certain extent in an animal exhibition.

No greater mistake could possibly be made. A man who purchases valuable race-horses does not ill-treat them or allow others to ill-treat them. On the contrary, apart from the humane point of view, he takes care that all the men in his establishment are kind to the animals in every way, attending to their wants and comforts, and taking the greatest care of them.

It is much the same in an animal exhibition. For instance, the lion has a market value determined by his ability as a performer. Any healthy, well-formed lion is worth from eight hundred to twelve hundred dollars, but in the case of a lion performing in a group, the loss of one means the practical disbandment of the group, because they have been taught to act in concert, and another will be necessary to take the place of the dead or disabled one. Add the lion's value to the cost of transportation and training, not to mention the costly item of feeding for years, and you will have a pretty large figure. It must, therefore, be apparent to those who will take the trouble to give the matter a little consideration, that the very greatest care must be taken of the animals, and that the slightest abuse of them cannot be allowed.

Even were this not so, I would not allow any one employed by me to stay another day

MLLE AURORA AND HER POLAR BEARS

if I once found that he was using any cruelty whatever to the animals in his charge. Kindness may not be appreciated by wild animals in one sense, but it undoubtedly tends to promote their comfort and health.

In feeding wild animals care is always taken to have the temperature of the food and water about the same as the temperature of the body. Should their meat or water be given to them too hot or too cold, it affects their stomachs, and they may be ill for weeks in consequence.

Only the very best and freshest of meat is given them. The least taint or disease would be sure to cause trouble in some form or other, and in many cases serious sickness and death would follow. It is true that lions in their wild state, when unable to procure fresh food, will occasionally eat tainted food. Whether or not their free, out-of-door life tends to counteract the ill effects of this, is not definitely known. All I personally know is, that lions and tigers in captivity are unable to eat any tainted food without a sickness following, which not only gives untold trouble and cost to the owners. but is also a source of extreme unpleasantness to those around. The only way to keep wild beasts wholesome and free from smell is to give them the best and freshest of food.

The best food for lions and tigers is good fresh beef or mutton, and an occasional sheep's head, of which they are extremely fond. Curiously enough, they are fond of any heads,—sheep's, chickens', calves', lambs', and others, —and will always eat them with the greatest relish. About twelve to fifteen pounds of beef or mutton are given to each of my lions and tigers twice a day, unless we deem it advisable to lessen it on any signs of sickness. Pork is never given under any circumstances, or much fat, although lions are rather fond of the fat of mutton.

With each piece of beef or mutton, if we can manage it, is given a piece of bone; the reason for this is that gnawing the bone helps digestion and is good for the teeth. On Sundays no food, but plenty of water, is given to the carnivora. This fast-day once a week is absolutely necessary; it rests their digestion, prevents them from growing too fat and lazy, and is beneficial to their health in many ways. I have carefully watched, and although at times some will get restless when feeding-time approaches on Sunday, they soon settle down again, and on Monday do not seem to be more hungry than on any other day in the week.

When it becomes apparent that a lion or tiger needs an aperient, a piece of liver is given, which has the desired effect. In some cases the liver is given once a week, particularly if the animal is a little off his feed. In other cases, a rabbit, pigeon, or chicken—always killed first—is given; this last food being specially beneficial should the animal be troubled with worms—a not unfrequent cause of sickness.

In cases of special sickness, of course, other means have to be employed, and special medicines given, in order to restore the animal to health. As all carnivora suffer, to a large extent, from the same complaints as human beings, they can be treated in much the same way.

When the sickness cannot be cured by a change of diet, a certain amount of medicine is mixed with the water or milk. Should the animal refuse to take it in this way, a tempting piece of fresh meat is plugged with the medicine, inserted in capsules, and in this way the animal takes his dose without tasting it.

But it is only in extreme cases that I consider it a good thing to give medicine. The best way is to let the animals fast for a time, give them plenty of fresh water, or a little milk, as much fresh air and exercise as possible, and leave the rest to Nature, which in nearly all cases effects a complete cure.

Bears are occasionally given raw meat, but it is not a good thing to give them too much. They thrive best on cooked meats, fish, and bread—dry or soaked in milk. A polar bear is extremely fond of fat pork, and would go through a great deal to get even a small bit; but one of the greatest delicacies you can give a polar bear is a dish of fish-oil. His relish and keen appreciation are well worth seeing, and no connoisseur could display greater enjoyment over a choice entrée than a polar bear over a dish of fish-oil.

Polar bears need special care in many ways.

The great change of climate is one of their worst trials, and there is no doubt that in the hot weather they suffer very much, no matter what one does for their comfort. Even in cold, frosty weather, a polar bear, when being trained, will get completely played out long before any ordinary bear would consider he had begun. In a very short time he will begin to pant and show signs of distress.

In training her group of polar bears, Mlle. Aurora took great pains to give the animals as little exertion as possible, and those who have seen this group perform will remember that the chief things they do are to take up positions on various stands and make pretty groupings. In this way she has certainly succeeded in getting one of the finest groups of polar bears on exhibition, while there is also the comforting feeling that the animals are not being made to do more than they are able.

One of the most interesting but, at the same time, uncertain things in the care of wild animals is the rearing and feeding of cubs. Cubs vary in size, health, strength, disposition, and temperament as much as children, and the care and treatment of them have to be regulated accordingly.

The mothers differ likewise. Many lionesses and tigresses make extremely good mothers, many do not. Some take the greatest care of their young, others appear to be absolutely indifferent, while a very few will even turn on their offspring and bite them viciously. The last case more often comes from worry or excitement; the mother is a little run down at the time, and unless absolute quiet is given her, she is apt to vent it on the little ones.

It will be readily understood that in an exhibition which is open to the public all day long it is extremely difficult to give any animal absolute quiet; but we always do our best, and it is wonderful how tender-hearted the roughest of men become toward the animals at a time like this. From the very commencement we try to make life as easy and comfortable as possible for the animal with young.

She is given an extra-roomy cage, placed where she will not be more disturbed than is necessary. Her health and diet are most carefully looked after, and she is watched continually. As soon as she appears uneasy, the cage is covered up, and she is left to herself until she has had plenty of time to settle down with her little ones. The cage is not opened to the public, as a rule, for two weeks, and even then great care has to be taken.

Should the cubs be fairly healthy, the mother takes care of them,—if she is a good mother,—and they remain with her for about eight or ten weeks, although the length of time depends entirely on the mother and the growth and well-being of the cubs. Weaning is begun gradually. At first the cubs are taken away from the mother in the morning and given back to her at night, and there are occasionally some very lively times during this episode, as it is an extremely dangerous proceeding to take the cubs away from the lioness or tigress. A small door is made in the cage, and while the mother's attention is attracted in another direction, the cubs are either coaxed out, or pushed through the door with an iron rod, and received in a basket or in the arms of one of the keepers.

When this takes place there is always a pathetic scene. The mother gives a peculiar moaning cry, low and short, as though breathless, while the cubs answer shrilly and make as much fuss and noise as they are able. The mother holds her head in the air when the cubs have disappeared, and listens eagerly for the direction from which the cries of her little ones come, and after answering with another moan tries to get out in the direction of the cries.

In the meantime the cubs are given a bone with a little piece of raw meat on it, generally beef. This takes up all their attention for the time being, and they will wrestle and tussle over these bones as though they had never known any other food. In this manner the day passes; but as evening comes on, the cubs become restless and cry pitifully, while the mother answers and listens attentively. When they are returned to the cage there is even more danger, for nothing will attract the mother's attention then. She knows her cubs are being brought nearer to her, and paces up and down, jumping up

LION MONARCHS IN INFANCY

toward the top of the cage, and doing her best in every possible way to get out.

As soon as the cubs are once inside again, she lies down on the floor, receiving them with great delight and giving little pleased cries of welcome, licking the cubs carefully all over, and playing with them; while the cubs jump about, roll over her, and show their pleasure in various ways. After this has happened a few times, the cubs have learned to eat meat, and sometimes, when the mother is fed, they will, by united efforts, drag her portion of meat away and fight over it, while she looks on, growling a little, but not interfering until they grow tired, when she carries it off and eats it quietly at her leisure.

When the cubs are taken away from the mother entirely, they are fed on soft food, milk, and an occasional bone, and soon begin to grow. One of the greatest dangers to which cubs are subject are convulsions, which appear to be partly caused by teething. In these cases certain specifics are given, the cub is kept in the animal infirmary as quietly as possible, and when it is better is returned to the other cubs. I have noticed frequently, and I have no doubt others have noticed also, that after convulsions cubs generally grow very fast, and in some cases appear even better and stronger than the others.

CHAPTER IV

THE FEEDING OF SNAKES AND ELEPHANTS

ALL wild beasts in their natural state will hunt and kill their food when hungry, and if too lazy to do this,—which is frequently the case with the lion,—they will keep a lookout for the remains of some other animal's "kill." When wild, animals always provide themselves with sufficient food, and appear to have many ways of working off a too heavy meal.

In captivity it is very different. They appear to lose their judgment to a certain extent, and in many cases will overfeed, if given the opportunity, or, in some instances, deliberately starve themselves for no accountable reason. This is specially the case with many snakes,— generally the larger ones,—and unless most carefully watched, they will literally starve themselves to death.

Snakes are difficult to feed; they appear to dislike being seen eating, and as they will not eat mammals or birds after rigor mortis has set in, great care is needed in feeding them. Pythons will sometimes go as long as eight or nine months without feeding, and when this is the case it is necessary to feed them by force.

Very few snakes, especially pythons, will allow themselves to be handled. At certain times, it is true, they will appear either indifferent or—if such a cool condition can be called friendliness—friendly toward their keepers; but this is, in nearly all cases, simply a sign that they are torpid from cold, and it merely needs the house to be heated a little to show not only that they can be very lively, but very spiteful and vindictive.

Occasionally, when some little operation is necessary, the snake has to be overpowered, but it is possible to do this only by numbers. No one man could do it; he would be crushed before he had time to turn around. The best way to set to work when the snake has deliberately refused to feed for many months is

"BRANDU," THE SNAKE-CHARMER

to wait until it is asleep. Then, at a given signal, several men pounce upon it—one grasps it by the back of its neck, several others stand on or hold different parts of its body, and others stand ready with rabbits, rats, and other small animals on the end of long poles, with which they force the food down the reptile's throat.

It is needless to say that some terrific tussles take place on these occasions, and often there is great danger. Unless the snake is quickly subdued, it is likely to subdue those who are molesting it; and even when several strong, able-bodied men are grasping it firmly, it will sometimes recoil with so much force and suddenness that the whole lot may be thrown to the ground.

The most dangerous part is when the moment comes for prying open its jaws. If this has been done safely, there comes the second difficulty of forcing food down its throat. There is no doubt that this process is objectionable and, in all probability, a little painful to the snake, and it is not to be wondered that at this moment it generally resists

4

with all its power. Even should the rabbit be got down the throat of the reptile, there is always the chance that it may be drawn out again with the pole. But this operation is generally performed successfully, and when the python has inside about a dozen rabbits, one or two guinea-pigs, and a few pigeons, he becomes heavy and sleepy, and at last settles down in a state of repletion from which he will probably not awaken for several days.

There have been many dangerous accidents from feeding snakes by force when they refuse food. Once a trainer entered and grasped a big python at the back of the neck, while several other men made ready to catch hold of it in other places. He caught it nicely in the right place, and was just speaking to the others when, to his horror, he found that the python had coiled itself firmly round his legs and body, and that he was unable to move.

With a great effort he shouted, and the men, realizing instantly what had happened, rushed forward and, with united efforts, uncoiled the monster, and so set him free. It was a matter of life and death, for in another moment the breath would have been crushed out of him, and he would have become a shapeless mass of flesh. It was only by his nerve and prompt call that he saved himself, for the men said afterward that until he shouted they were not aware of what the snake had done. After this nothing would ever induce that trainer to have anything to do with snakes again. He said he could never forget the feeling of unspeakable horror and indefinable helplessness he experienced when the coils were encircling him.

At another time, a young pig was thrown to a pair of snakes. In this case the snakes were ravenously hungry, and, consequently, very lively. The larger one of the two darted for it, but the smaller snake was too quick for him, and had swallowed the pig whole before the other could touch it.

Now followed a very curious incident, and one which, I believe, has not often been observed. The large snake waited until another pig was thrown in, and took care this time to get it, but immediately after swallowing it deliberately turned to the small snake and swallowed him, swollen as he was with the first pig. This snake lay in a state of repletion after this for weeks, and from various indications that we had I don't fancy that his cannibalism agreed with him.

But a more curious incident than either of these occurred at the Pan-American Exhibition with Great Peter, the largest python ever kept in captivity. Great Peter had been fasting for some time,—most of the summer, in fact,—and we were beginning to feel anxious about him, when, toward the end of September, he suddenly became very lively—always a sure sign of hunger.

Much delighted at these signs, his keeper at once looked for suitable food for him, and procured a young razor-back pig. As a general rule, all animals when put in with snakes are rendered helpless by fear. They appear to be paralyzed by a strange fascination, and instead of making the slightest resistance or attempt to get away, stay on the very spot where they are thrown until the snake kills them with a bite or thrusts them into their living tomb by swallowing them.

M. JOHNSON AND HIS TRAINED ELEPHANT

But this little razorback was made of different stuff, and was neither fascinated nor helpless from fear. The moment he entered the cage it was evident that he meant to have a good fight for it, no matter what happened. He gave the python no time to spring, but, taking time by the forelock, ran up to the huge snake, screaming shrilly at the top of his voice, and fastened his sturdy tusks firmly in the back of the snake's neck.

He squealed no more after this, but attended strictly to business, and hung on like grim death. There was a momentary pause, and then the daring little pig shook his enemy vigorously as he would a rat. For a second or two over thirty-two feet of python coiled and lashed about the cage in a furious manner, but the pig hung on.

His triumph was not long. The contest was too unequal. Suddenly the thick coils left the air, and, descending on the plucky little animal, coiled round and round, crushing his body and cracking his ribs as though they were nutshells. But still the pig hung on,— hung on until the coils of the snake gradually relaxed,—and then, as they loosened weakly and fell off, the pig, game to the last, dropped off the python's neck, dead. His enemy lay quietly beside him—the conqueror and the conquered together.

Had the razorback only allowed himself to give one little squeal when he was being crushed, he would have been obliged to let go his hold and we might have saved the python, but his pluckiness cost us a valuable reptile.

Elephants are big feeders, and few realize the quantity of food they need. A fair-sized elephant in a healthy condition will consume on an average about two hundred pounds of hay, a bushel of oats, and six or eight loaves of bread a day. This is in addition to all the other things in the way of peanuts, cakes, crackers, nuts, etc., it gets from the visitors. Occasionally one or two large basketsful of fresh vegetables are given to each one, for elephants are fond of any vegetables, fruits, or grain, and nearly always seem to be hungry.

From this a rough estimate can be gathered of the vast quantity of food it is necessary to provide for a group of only half a dozen ele-

phants. The difficulties are often considerable, especially in small country places where the produce is not equal to the demand. It will often take one or two men all their time to procure enough food to keep the animals even in fair condition. Grain can generally be had, but too much grain is not good for them, and the necessity for a variety, which is not always obtainable, causes much difficulty.

Elephants are not particularly strong or robust constitutionally. They suffer from various ailments in captivity, even with the greatest care. Colds and chills are the most frequent, and, though not themselves dangerous, they sometimes lead to pneumonia, and when once an elephant has pneumonia he never recovers.

It is almost impossible to give an elephant medicine. Every way has been tried, but in many cases to no purpose. The moment he tastes it nothing will induce him to swallow it, and he promptly spits it out. Capsules have been tried, in the hope that the animal would swallow them whole, but he at once crushed them with his teeth, and at the first taste the usual spitting out took place. Medicine has also been introduced into loaves of bread and drinks of water or milk, but the elephant detected it at once, and it was, of course, absolutely impossible to force it down his throat, as can be done with some of the other animals.

About the only possible thing to make an elephant take when he has a bad cold is a good dose of hot whisky and onions, and he appears not only to like it but to wish for more. However, if elephants are looked after and cared for properly, it is rarely necessary to give them medicine. They are generally healthy, and the chief thing to guard against is a chill or cold, when there is always the possibility of pneumonia following.

An elephant sleeps in a peculiar manner. Nearly all lie on their left sides with their trunks curled up, making a peculiar hissing noise at regular intervals, something like the sound of steam issuing from a kettle. He is not a sound sleeper. He does not take much notice of his keeper prowling round in the night, but should anything strange or unusual take place, the hissing stops suddenly, two

small, red lights appear in the elephant's head, and the animal is wide awake and evidently watching. At the first sign of danger he trumpets shrilly, so that oftentimes he gives the first alarm, when no living thing besides suspects anything amiss.

CHAPTER V

CHARACTERISTICS OF DIFFERENT ANIMALS

IT must not be supposed that all captive felines are amenable to education. The personal equation enters in very largely. What
will do for the lion may do for the tiger, the
leopard, the puma, or the jaguar; but what
will do for one lion may not do for another,
nor can all tigers or leopards be trained alike.
Many, in assuming that the lion is brave and
the tiger treacherous, and in ascribing set
qualities to the others, are generalizing without basis.

The lion is feared for his clumsiness as
much as anything, because it makes him likely
to do serious damage unwittingly; the jaguar
and leopard for their terrible swiftness in action; and the tiger for a tenacity of purpose
which, when once aroused, is almost uncon-

querable. But it cannot be said in general that one is more to be feared than another. It is the individual that must be reckoned with by the successful trainer.

One animal may be of a heavy, phlegmatic disposition; another may be slow and stupid; a third subject to fits of unreasonable and ungovernable rage; another curious and inquisitive, making him incessantly restless; another nervous and timid; and yet another will show a fussy and irritable disposition, and refuse to perform unless all the circumstances are just as he considers they should be.

With rare exceptions, all the felines are untrustworthy and more or less treacherous, and no matter how long they may have been trained, or how well their trainer may know them, they are liable at any moment, and without the least reason, to turn on him. Each one has his characteristics, and it is these special characteristics which require such extremely careful study and continual watching.

Weather affects wild animals in just the same way in which it affects human beings. This appears to be the case specially with lions. Damp, muggy weather will make them seemingly depressed and irritable, and in this state they are doubly unwilling to do anything they do not feel inclined to. In hot weather they become lazy and sleepy, and it is sometimes with the greatest difficulty that any of the lions can be made to perform. This laziness is natural. In his native state the lion sleeps all day, and will only go out for food at night when urged by hunger.

In cold weather, Captain Bonavita finds his lions so frisky and playful that it is extremely dangerous to make them perform, for a playful lion is a terrible thing—with even a tap from one of his paws he can break the neck of a horse.

One cold, frosty day, when Captain Bonavita was trying to get his lions to perform, one, a huge beast, was particularly playful, and, in spite of all his care, at last got one claw in the cloth of his coat. In a moment the animal dragged him to the ground, and, not being able to get his claw free,—as it had caught in the cloth,—became wildly enraged. Had it not been that one of the men outside the cage

THE OLD ARM-CHAIR

gave the trainer an opportunity to cut the cloth, he would have lost his life in a few minutes.

Apart from all these physical variations, the peculiarities of temperament also must be studied and watched. Each animal is so different from its fellows and so subject to sudden changes of temper, that this requires the most careful observation; nor can any reason often be found for their different actions.

There is a very famous lion now performing who fears but one thing: a stick in the left hand. The trainer may have a club, a whip, a knife, a pistol, or even a firebrand in his right hand, and the lion will spring for him fearlessly, but the smallest thing in the left hand will keep the animal perfectly tractable. No satisfactory explanation of this individual peculiarity has ever been offered, and one trainer limps for life simply because he did not make the discovery in time.

Lions have no affection; they become used to and tolerant of their trainers, and their obedience and docility is partly, if not wholly, due to ignorance and to the dread of anything they do not comprehend. They seemingly do not understand why the trainers are not afraid of them, and do not appear to realize that one little blow could put them out of existence. It is only when they lose respect for their trainer—either because he has contracted bad habits, or because he has been foolish or unguarded enough at some time to let them see that he was nervous—that they realize that he is only a small thing compared to themselves, and turn on him.

The great majority of cases of defense of a trainer by an animal have little foundation, other than the minds of the ingenious press agent. But there have been rare cases where animals have conceived a real affection for a trainer, and fawned upon him like a dog, and even protected him from others when they attacked him.

One such case concerned Mme. Pianka. During a rehearsal at St. Louis several years ago, she was suddenly attacked by a young lion and thrown to the floor. Instantly, a smaller lioness, of whom she was particularly fond and who had appeared to return the affection, leaped upon the lion and gave him so much to attend to that the trainer got to her feet, and was then able to whip the offending lion back to his corner. No trainer, however, depends on such interference; in fact, he knows and takes it for granted that if he is attacked and thrown, the other beasts in the cage will join in only too quickly.

The fellowship of animal for animal in the bonds of slavery is stronger than that of animal for man. Once in the cage, the trainer is alone among vastly superior forces that at any moment may become hostile, and his wisest plan is always to mistrust and look out, and not to expect anything but united hostility should he slip or be attacked.

An animal seldom, if ever, attacks a trainer for blood or a desire for meat. The danger lies in the instinct of ferocity; and many experiments made in this direction undoubtedly prove that animals attack from inherent fierceness and savagery alone. A tiger will occasionally show a desire for blood, but other animals very seldom.

I made an experiment some years ago in

order to see whether civilized food would make any difference in the nature of a wild animal. I had a fine, well-grown young lion, which I reared for two years on cooked food —boiled meat and vegetables. He had never tasted blood or raw meat, and yet when he was a little over two and a half years old he broke out and killed a fine young buck which was loose in the runway behind the cage; and when in the arena afterward, proved to be no different in any way from the other animals who had been brought up on raw steaks and other fresh meat.

It is doubtful whether lions, tigers, and their kin have minds developed in a wild state to anything like the degree attained by those of the smaller fur-bearing animals, such as ermine, fox, wolverene, or a number of the smaller rodents. They are endowed with so much agility, strength, and endurance that they need hardly exercise much thought in securing their livelihood; while the caution and ingenuity required of the weaker species, in order not only to get food, but also to escape from their enemies, tend to sharpen their faculties daily.

MADAME PIANKA

The only enemy feared by the larger wild beasts is man. Why they should feel this supreme awe of man it is difficult to explain. Neither his size nor his erect position can account for it, and it is only in long settled and much frequented regions that his firearms are dreaded. The explanation probably is that they are unable to comprehend his habits, to fathom his mental attitude, to learn what he is likely to do next, and are awed by the mystery of his conduct, as we might be by that of some supernatural being of unknown power who came among us and threatened our liberty and our happiness.

The minds of the great carnivora are little exercised in nature, and do not develop. Accustomed to seeing all the denizens of the forest quail before them, they do not know what it is to feel a sense of help needed or of favors granted. It is perfectly natural, then, that trainers should say that kindness is not appreciated by them. A tigress is, in most cases, as likely to eat up her keeper after six years of attention as she would be after six days, should she consider that she were safe in doing so.

5

A quiet tiger is always to be feared and watched carefully. Mr. Charles Miller, who has been so successful in training the fiercest Bengal tigers, has no fear of the noisy ones, who are forever growling, snarling, and spitting defiance; but of the others, who are stealthily quiet and show in no way by voice or gesture that they object to what he has to do, he takes the greatest care and caution. Whenever he is obliged to turn his back on one of these tigers, he takes care to turn it on the snarling ones, who do nothing but make a noise. The quiet ones are only waiting for the very first opportunity to spring, and one spring from a tiger is fatal. In one performance, Mr. Miller turned his head quickly to find a treacherous animal crawling stealthily on his stomach toward him. The instant the tiger saw he was noticed he stopped, and began to lick his paws in the most indifferent manner, but the next moment he was trying to do the same thing again, until brought smartly up by a flick of the whip. This he also took quietly, although with a curious hiss. He was simply biding his time.

It is an acknowledged fact, among those who know anything about wild animals, that continual quietness invariably goes with a mean or savage nature, and that the animal who does not snarl should be carefully watched at all times by those who have anything to do with him. Why this should be an indication it is impossible, at least for me, to say. I have studied the matter very carefully, and many of the cleverest trainers and owners of wild animals have done the same.

As a rule, lions are much slower than lionesses. They are far more deliberate in their movements, and, consequently, seem more haughty and majestic. A lioness will frisk and romp about even when she has had several families, but a full-grown lion will seldom, if ever, depart in the slightest from his habitual grave, solemn manner. Generally speaking, the female felines are more easily managed and not as dangerous as the males, but they are always crafty and treacherous, and the time when they appear to be indifferent or off their guard is the time to be more than usually cautious.

There are, of course, cases where the females act swiftly and suddenly without treacherous motives, and this makes them even more dangerous, because one never can tell when this may happen. At Philadelphia, some years ago, we had an illustration of this, and of what a terrible and lightning-like blow a jaguar can give.

This jaguar, a magnificent female, had been rehearsing some fancy leap from shelf to shelf, and as a finale was to jump from a projection from the side of the cage, about seven feet high, to a wooden ball some ten feet distant, and maintain herself upon the ball until a given signal from the trainer—a most difficult feat. The graceful creature measured the distance carefully for a few moments, keeping her eyes fixed on the ball, and stretched her slender neck forward toward the goal before essaying the leap.

Then she launched herself. That leap was a study in beauty of form and grace of motion, but there was a slight miscalculation. The jaguar landed on the ball, but after clinging desperately for a moment to the oscillating

sphere, fell to the ground, landing in a crouching attitude. Swifter than the eye could follow, there was a motion of the paw, and the
wooden ball, weighing nearly a hundred
pounds, sailed across the stage and hit the
bars with an impact that shook the entire
structure as an earthquake would have done,
frightening the pair of lions and the leopard
who shared the cage almost to a frenzy.

As for the jaguar, she glared fiercely round
with a hiss and snarl, as though to see whether
any of the others were laughing at her, and
then slunk away to one side, where she ex-
amined her paw with an appearance of solici-
tude, listening meanwhile to the rebukes of the
trainer with obvious confusion. It is the possibility that at any moment a blow of that
caliber may land on him, which effectually
prevents the trainer from experiencing any
feelings of ennui when in the cage with wild
animals.

Elephants have their little peculiarities, like
all other animals, and one of them is their
strange and often unaccountable antipathy to
some persons, and their warm affection for

others. One of my elephants is of a most gentle disposition, but hates the sight of a dog. A tiny toy terrier is enough to drive him nearly frantic, and unless the animal is removed at once he would kill him instantly, for an elephant makes up his mind quickly.

The majority of wild animals appear to be fond of music, although a great many dislike it extremely. As a rule, the large carnivora seem to like it, and the trained animals will often rouse themselves at the sound and look round inquiringly. There is no doubt whatever that it is a stimulus to them. In many cases it is their principal cue, and without it they are uncertain, restless, and unhappy.

Some time ago the band of a traveling show went on strike in the middle of a performance, and left in a body. Three trained tigers were the next feature on the program. When they came on they looked inquiringly at the orchestra for the music, and then two of them quietly settled down on their haunches and refused to go on. The third, who was of less experience, made a feeble start and then joined his companions on strike. Orders, commands, threats, and flickings of the whip were useless. No music, no performance, was obviously the motto of these tigers; and they stuck to it until finally the trainer, finding that to try to force them further was dangerous, was obliged to let them return to their cage without giving any performance at all.

The trainer feared that he would never get them to perform again, for once let an animal off his performance and it generally means that he expects and insists on not giving any more exhibitions at all. However, the next day, when the differences with the musicians had been settled, and the tigers were brought out again, they seemed perfectly satisfied as soon as they heard the music, and acquitted themselves better than ever.

One incident which has always puzzled my trainers and myself occurred with a fine, full-grown Barbary lion. When the band has been playing a certain set of tunes for some time, it will naturally change them for newer and more popular ones. I have never noticed that the animals were aware of it, but in this case there was one tune which this particular lion did not like. The moment it was started he grew restless and uneasy, moaned and whimpered, and finally roared to such a degree that we could not imagine what was the matter with him.

This went on day after day and night after night, until at last we noticed that he always did it about the same time, and finally, when the tunes were changed about a little, that he always did it when a particular tune was being played. We tried him the next morning, at quite a different hour, with the same tune, and it had the same effect. The moment it was started he would get up, moan, whimper, snarl, and grow more and more uneasy, until he worked himself up into a rage and roared at the top of his voice, which was strong even for a lion.

The music appeared to irritate his nerves. Whether this was so or not I cannot tell, but it evidently annoyed him to a painful degree. After making sure of this fact, I ordered that tune to be left out for the future, and from that time to this he has never shown dislike to any other music, and is quiet and peaceable, and a good performer.

MR. CHARLES MILLER AND HIS BENGAL TIGERS

CHAPTER VI

"GOING BAD"—ANIMAL INSTINCT

WHAT those who have charge of wild animals in captivity, and especially trainers, dread most among the large carnivora, is that inexplicable change of temperament on the part of the animal known in the parlance of the menagerie as "going bad." Lions are likely to go bad about the tenth year of life; tigers two or three years earlier. The male tiger is the dread of the profession when he reaches this condition, because he is more likely to go into a frenzy without warning, and, once gone bad, nothing will satisfy him but murder. He will leap for any man within reach, and when once his teeth are on the bone, nothing but fire will make him relinquish it, and not always that.

This " going bad " may come in the nature

of a sudden attack, or it may develop slowly and be counteracted if taken in time. An old trainer can usually detect the symptoms of this curious ailment. It seems to be in the nature of a disease, and other animals recognize it and shun the affected one. When its progress is apparent the danger is not great; all that is required then is a level head, and the wisdom to refrain from further interference with the animal.

A good trainer never dreams of interfering with an animal in this condition. If attacked, his one aim is to defend himself, until he has a chance to escape from the cage, and to separate the animal from his fellows as soon as possible. Sometimes this bad temper will last but a short time, and again it will become the permanent condition of the animal. In that case he is sent to the lonely cage to spend the rest of his life in comparative obscurity, disturbed merely by the passing crowd and his daily meals.

Let an animal once acquire a love for blood and he is spoiled for the rest of his life. If the killing instinct once develops it can rarely be eradicated. Rajah, a tiger which has already killed two men, and severely injured me on more than one occasion, "went bad" suddenly, and his taste for blood having once been aroused, it would have been worse than useless to attempt to do anything with him again, and he is now kept carefully by himself. Formerly, he was one of the best trick tigers before the public, but some unknown thing ruffled his nature, he gained a realization of his own brute strength and a taste for blood, and his career as a performer was over.

As a rule, a trainer can also tell when the critical moment has come in this peculiar phase of "going bad." The man who puts his head in a lion's mouth, sooner or later, arrives at the point where he feels that to continue would endanger his life. A trainer once had an experience of that kind in England.

He had safely accomplished the hazardous feat for several months without any particular feeling of trepidation. One night he placed his head in the lion's mouth as usual, and was about to draw it out again when he suddenly had a shuddering, indefinable realization that the lion's good temper was gone. He knew the danger, and prepared for it by bracing all his strength against that of the lion's jaws.

He removed his head slowly, as usual, for the least hurry might have provoked an attack, but in a second the lion snapped at him while his face was yet within danger. The tip of his chin was caught and lacerated. That was the conclusion of the act with that lion, and he was relegated to solitude like others troubled with the same complaint.

Elephants also " go bad," and there is even more danger with these huge beasts than with lions and tigers; for they may break out and kill and injure a great number of people, besides causing an immense amount of damage by tearing up and destroying property.

Most people have heard how many valuable elephants have had to be killed owing to their becoming " rogues." A rogue elephant is a terrible creature in more ways than one, for his huge bulk and enormous strength make him not only a formidable enemy, but his cunning and viciousness can be appreciated only by those who have come in constant contact with him.

There appears to be no special age for an elephant going bad, but the majority of these animals become dangerous after a certain time in captivity. The most tractable and gentle elephant I ever had suddenly " went bad " for no conceivable reason, and although after much coaxing and soothing he appeared to settle down quietly, there were certain indications soon after that he intended mischief. Finally, his small eyes became so red and threatening that I considered it wiser to have him killed, rather than run any risk of his sacrificing human lives.

With regard to the instincts of animals, I have had some very curious experiences. Just before a disastrous fire at Baltimore, when nearly all the poor animals were terribly burned, many in the exhibition noticed how restless and uneasy the animals were, but as there appeared to be no reason for it, we thought nothing more about it.

When the time for the performance came, not one of the animals would move out of its cage. It is not unusual for wild animals to get restless fits sometimes, but it is extremely unusual for them all, at one and the same time, absolutely to refuse to come out of their cages at the command of the trainers. The majority of wild-animal trainers are superstitious, and many of them began to wonder what it meant and whether it was a bad omen, for not one in the whole building had the slightest idea that the fire was even then gaining ground.

There was not the faintest smell of smoke or any other indication to give warning that one of the greatest calamities I ever had was just coming upon me. Not more than a quarter of an hour before the men had been round, according to the usual custom, to see that everything was safe and in good order, but nothing was noticed out of the way, and until the flames suddenly burst forth no one had any idea that there was the least danger or trouble at hand.

Another curious instance of animal instinct occurred in the winter of 1902–03 at Ocala, Florida. Mme. Pianka had taken her lions there to perform, and as soon as they arrived every one noticed that the animals, especially the lions, were restless and uneasy at night, and that they behaved very strangely.

It is customary, soon after arriving at a place, to turn the animals out into the steel arena for exercise, as, of course, it is quite impossible to give them any exercise at all while on a long journey. The moment the lions entered the arena, instead of stretching themselves luxuriously and pacing up and down in their usual manner, they stopped short, with ears back and noses to the ground, and commenced to sniff in the most peculiar manner.

It was impossible to rouse them up or make them move about. Each one would walk a few paces, but always with his head bent down and sniffing the ground. When the time for the performance came on, their behavior was still more curious. These lions were Mme. Pianka's favorites, and as she had always been very fond of them, and had had them in training for several years, she had been accustomed to caress them. Although the majority of them took this in the grave, dignified manner peculiar to lions, one or two had appeared actually to like her endearments, and had occasionally rubbed their huge heads against her face.

But at this time they would not let her touch them. Each one let her know that she must keep her distance, or it would be a serious matter. Neither would they perform at the accustomed words of command. Indeed, their manner grew so forbidding and dangerous that at last she dared not even go near them.

That same night Mme. Pianka was awakened by the watchman calling to say that the lions were digging large holes in the ground, and that he thought, at the rate they were working, they would very soon dig themselves out altogether. All the assistants were called up, the electric lights were turned on, and it was found that the lions had already dug holes deep enough in the earth to bury themselves.

The danger was doubly great because so unexpected. Hyenas and wolves will dig holes in the ground in this manner, but for lions to do so is almost unheard of. The lions were with great difficulty taken out of the cage, with evident reluctance on their part, and put

QUEER FRIENDS—CAMEL, LIONESSES, AND DROMEDARY

once more into their traveling compartments. The ground was securely battened down and covered thickly with fine sand, disinfectant, and sawdust.

The following night the lions were turned into the arena again, but in a very short time they had scratched away the sand and sawdust and dug up the earth, and it was only just in time that the lions were once more removed to their traveling-cages in exceedingly ugly and dangerous moods.

Many solutions were offered by various people,—especially by those who knew nothing whatever about animals,—but no satisfactory one could be found. We thought of the change of climate, of air, scene, and food. The lions had grown accustomed to changes of air and climate, and the food was the same kind that they had been accustomed to in captivity. We next thought of the water; but it was pure and good, and there seemed to be no accounting for this strange freak on the part of the animals. Had one or two shown this peculiar propensity, we should naturally have concluded that they had "gone bad," but as all

6

were doing the same thing, and two were quite young lions, this could not be the case.

At last this was mentioned to the chief of police and one or two old residents, and we then discovered that the tent had been pitched directly over an old graveyard in Ocala, and although most of the bodies had been removed, there was, of course, every probability that some of the remains were still under the ground.

This, of course, solved the mystery, to our great relief; for, having found out the cause, we very soon applied a remedy, and it was not long before we had the tent and the animals removed some distance off. As soon as the animals were removed, their savage sulkiness vanished, and they at once settled down into their old routine, and were as obedient and good-natured as they had ever been.

CHAPTER VII

HOW WILD ANIMALS ARE CAPTURED

FEW who see wild animals in cages realize the vast amount of trouble, danger, and expense necessary to get them there. The greatest danger lies in capturing the animals in their native countries.

It is an easy task to hunt wild animals for sport, compared to the difficulties connected with their capture, not only alive, but uninjured. An injured animal is rarely any use. The injuries, added to the frenzy of a wild animal when first caught, leave very little chance of his surviving the ordeal, even for a few days; and should he do so, the chances are that he will remain in such a miserable state for so long that he will not repay the cost of capture, feeding, and transportation.

As a rule, although rare specimens have

been made exceptions, an injured animal is either killed at once, or, if there should appear to be no immediate danger to the lives of his captors, is allowed to escape.

The chief danger lies, not so much when face to face with the animals, but when hunting and tracking them. The wariest and most careful hunter may be tracking an animal, and at the same time be tracked by the very animal he is seeking, who may spring on him at any moment.

There is no more ticklish or dangerous task than tracking lions in the vast Nubian deserts. The scorching sun pours down with such force that few men can stand it. The effect on the eyes is blinding. There is little or no shade, with the exception of occasional small palm-trees and bushes, while the jutting rocks afford splendid hiding-places for the king of beasts.

It may happen that when a lion-hunt has been formed an elephant or a rhinoceros appears, and either of these animals in their wild state presents a difficult problem. A rogue elephant will put a whole crowd of lion-

WILD ASS, QUAGGA, AND ZEBRAS

hunters to rout, and clear that part of the country of men for some little time to come. A rhinoceros is also a formidable foe. Although comparatively slow-moving, it can, when excited, move quite quickly enough, and its horns can be used with terrible effect.

In capturing animals alive, it is generally considered better to get young ones. A number of natives form parties and then go in different directions, until they come upon the spoor of either a lioness or young lions. They then signal to one another by peculiar calls, and, meeting together, follow up the trail until they find the lair.

Should they find that the lair contains a lioness and cubs, they do all they can to induce the lioness to come out, and if unable to capture her alive, shoot her and then capture the cubs. This sounds very simple, but a lioness with cubs is one of the most savage of animals, and she will fight to the last. Having killed the lioness, there is still danger with the cubs; for lion cubs are fierce, strong, and vicious creatures, and can tear and bite with their claws and teeth in a terrible manner.

One plan is to throw nets or a piece of strong sackcloth over the young ones, in which they become entangled. The men then run forward, pick them up, and carry them off, and they are extremely lucky if they escape with a few scratches only, for the cubs, though tangled in the net, are able to make an exceedingly lively fight. Sometimes the lioness is not wounded fatally, and she is then far more dangerous than before. It is quite impossible to take the cubs in that case, for she would follow for miles, and in addition to making the cubs more savage, her cries of pain and distress would be more than likely to bring out her mate from some neighboring hiding-place, and then nothing could be done but to drop the cubs and withstand the lions' attack.

When the cubs are captured, goats are obtained in full milk, and the cubs are fed by them until they are past the first teething-stage and able to eat meat. In some cases spaniels are provided as foster-mothers, and although at first the dogs are uneasy at their somewhat rough and savage foster-children, they generally grow fond of them, and the affection is more often than not returned by the cubs.

For catching full-grown lions large traps of various forms are used. One trap is square, one of the sides lifting up on a spring, like the old-fashioned mouse-trap. This trap is baited with a piece of fresh meat, and as soon as the lion has entered the trap the door shuts down and he is a prisoner. But lions are shrewd and cunning, like all the cat tribe, and many a man has lost his life by going to look at a baited trap.

Many cases have been known where a lion, becoming suspicious, resisted the temptation of the fresh meat, and lay down in hiding and kept watch. When the rash hunter came to see whether the bait had been touched, the lion sprang on him, preferring fresh man-meat to the bait inside the trap. In one case the lid went down, but, in some way or other, one of the paws of the lion was caught in it, and when the men came to look at him, by a wonderful feat of strength he raised the lid and sprang out, killing two of them.

Animals are also captured by driving them

with torches or fire into inclosures made with bamboo rods and nets. When in these inclosures the animals are fairly secure, as any attempt to climb over the bamboo rods only sends them back into the nets, the bamboo not being sufficiently strong to bear their weight. The animals are generally kept a little while without food until they become somewhat subdued, and are then taken to their places of transportation.

In India the natives catch tigers by a peculiar method. The leaves of the sycamore and the large plantain are smeared with a sticky substance and left in the trail of the tiger. The moment the animal puts his foot on one of these leaves he immediately rubs it over his head, in order to get rid of it. This naturally makes his head sticky and uncomfortable, which causes him to roll on the ground. By doing this he becomes covered with the leaves, and when he is mad with rage the natives come cautiously up and cover him with strong nets and sacking.

In other parts of Asia the animals are caught in various ways,—some in pitfalls and traps, and some by meat baited in such a cunning manner that a native is able either to wound or to capture the animal while he is eating it. In running through the forests, the animals pass over these traps, which are carefully concealed by branches and limbs of trees, fall in, and are prisoners. In many cases the animals are so terrified that they die of fright; in others, they absolutely refuse to eat, and die soon after capture. Sometimes the captured animals die just when the cost of transportation has been paid, and it is then discovered that they had been injured internally in falling. In most cases, however, they are kept without food for a short time, and when they have quieted down a little some meat is thrown in to them, and they soon become accustomed to their surroundings.

Elephants are generally caught in nooses, or by being driven into a keddah. A number of men surround the elephant, and forming a circle of fire, which they make smaller and smaller, compel him to go into the keddah. He is then roped to some strong logs and allowed to remain in that state until quiet, when a tame elephant leads him about until he becomes tractable. Some elephants can never be tamed, and in this case it is generally considered wiser either to kill the animal or to let him have his freedom again.

In catching snakes various devices are used, but all methods are attended with a certain amount of danger. One way is to set the grass on fire in a circle where it is known that snakes have their hiding-places. This will always bring them out, and they naturally rush from the fire. As they rush out, they are caught in large nets mounted on wooden hoops to which is attached a large bag.

As the reptiles are generally stupefied with the smoke, it is not a difficult thing to those accustomed to the task to drop them into the bag. They are then carried to the packing-station, where they are packed in boxes and sent direct to Europe.

While on the journey, neither food nor water is given them; the chief things are warmth and freedom from damp. Cold is dangerous to all snakes; it not only makes them dull and torpid, but causes them to have mouth disease, from which they never recover; and as some of them are extremely valuable, this point is very important. Many instances have been known where a whole collection of valuable snakes have been found dead on arrival.

CHAPTER VIII

THE WILD ANIMALS' KINDERGARTEN

AN animal learns by association. Though it is a common belief, fear is not the reason for his obedience to the trainer's commands. Habit and ignorance are what cause the animal to become an apt pupil in the hands of the trainer. The animal becomes accustomed to the same way of doing the same things at much the same time, and ignorance of his own power keeps him in this state of subjection.

This habit is developed in the animal by a laborious and patient process, and it requires an intimate knowledge of animal nature to perfect it. The easiest animal to train is one that is born in his native haunts and new to captivity. The reason is obvious. The one bred in captivity has nothing to fear from

TEACHING A LION TO RIDE A TRICYCLE

man, and knows his own strength and the
fear he inspires. Accustomed from earliest
infancy to the greatest care and coddling, he
arrives one day at the stage of growth where
he realizes the value of his own claws, for the
use of them has shown him that human beings
do not like to be scratched. Some attendant,
who has, perhaps, been playing with him day
by day, admiring his pretty, innocent-looking
little face, soft furry body, and velvety paws
while he is still a mere cub, drops him suddenly one day when he feels the deep prick
of the claws hidden in those paws. The next
time some one comes along, the cub may not
be in the mood for handling; he remembers
his past experience, that scratching means
" let go," and he puts this into practice. His
liberty is promptly secured, and he lies in peace
in his cage.

The next man who comes may get a deeper
scratch, and he lets the cub alone even more
severely, a fact that the cub notes and remembers the next time, for he is gradually acquiring a deeper disrespect for man and his
puerile ways; he is beginning to know the

value of the little knives he carries sheathed in those paws, and he is very soon autocratic in his independence. He accepts his food as tribute and his care as homage due, and regards man simply as another and much weaker animal.

Such an animal is difficult to train. The only method that may be pursued at all is severe letting alone for several years. All that time he holds himself more and more aloof. He is, in a way, congratulating himself on his success, and man in time becomes a shadowy being who periodically brings his food, and who, in some inexplicable way, keeps him in that oblong box for people to stare at.

He does not mind the people, nor does he mind the cage very much, for he has never known anything else; but deep in him—so deep that he barely realizes its existence—slumbers a desire for freedom and an unutterable longing for the blue sky and the free air. Man, in some way, is to blame for that intangible "something" that he wants, and scarcely knows that he wants; and man has shown him that he is afraid of his claws. and. therefore.

the animal hates and despises man and all belonging to him.

The cub grows insolent in his haughtiness; then his undefined desire for freedom decreases somewhat, becomes more and more vague, and his existence is finally comprised in just two sensations: eating and sleeping. The disturbance of either is an insult, and any one who disturbs either an enemy. Man allows both to continue, and so the cub in his arrogance tolerates him.

The cub passes beyond his days of cubhood, and acquires almost the years and stature of a full-grown lion. He has few of the qualities of the newly captured animal. He does not fear man; he knows his own power. He regards man, as an inferior, with an attitude of disdain and silent hauteur.

When it is considered that his memory of the days when scratching insured independence has faded, his training is begun. He meets it with a reserved majesty and silent indifference, as though he had a dumb realization of his wrongs.

He has probably been in a large cage. This

is changed to a smaller one that has movable bars. The bars are fitted in this way for a definite purpose. Until now the lion has kept in the rear of his cage, as far as possible from the man who feeds him, grabbing his meat and retreating with a sullen growl. It is desired to bring him into closer relationship with his would-be trainer.

The bars are moved day by day. Soon the cage is small enough to permit a fairly long stick to reach from the front to the back. Such a stick, in the hands of a man, is introduced and allowed to remain several hours. The lion may take no notice of it; he may growl and he may grab it. Whatever he does, the stick is kept there and replaced if destroyed. When he has grown accustomed to the stick, it is gently rubbed along his neck and back. Though he snaps at it at first, when once he finds that the stroking is a pleasure, he soon allows it to be done without any protest.

Sometimes a piece of meat is put at the end of the stick by the trainer, and this is found to act as an inducement to allow the stick to come

POLAR BEAR USED AT PAN-AMERICAN EXPOSITION FOR DRAWING
CHILDREN'S CARRIAGE

close to the animal. Very often the lion will crunch the stick to splinters, and this the trainer allows, as he wishes to prove to the animal that he has nothing to fear from the stick itself. In a very short time he takes the meat quietly, without even growling at the stick; and when this stage of the proceedings is reached the stick is made shorter each day, until finally it is not much longer than the hand.

As a rule, when once the stick trick has been accomplished with an animal, it is comparatively easy to get on a little farther, for by that time the animal not only has no objection to the presence of the trainer, but appears to look for him and expect him. His objections, suspicions, and resentment disappear, and very soon the fingers replace the stick in the stroking process, and, being softer and more soothing than the stick, seem to give greater pleasure than the wood. This is a great step taken, for one of the most difficult things is to get any wild animal to allow himself to be touched with the human hand.

With a lion which comes straight from

Africa or Asia, the case is different. Lions are usually trained when between two and three years of age. A two-year-old of fine physique and restless nature has been brought straight from his native haunts. There he has been actually the monarch of the jungle. His life has been free and fearless.

Suddenly, in the midst of his regal existence, he falls into a hidden pit or is snared in the woods. His desperate struggles, his rage and gnashing of teeth, all the force of his tremendous strength, are ineffectual in breaking the bonds of his captivity.

After his first supreme efforts are over and he has thoroughly exhausted himself, he proves himself a very king of beasts in his haughty disdain. He apparently realizes his helplessness and submits to everything in sullen, dignified silence.

The lion comes to the trainer from the jungle, after having been subjected to abuse and gross indignities. From the time of his capture by natives who have neither feeling nor consideration for the poor animal, until he reaches his final quarters, his treatment, as a rule, is such as to terrify him and render him nervous in the extreme.

He has been kept in cramped quarters, cruelly joggled and crushed in a narrow box, while on his way to the coast from the interior, his bedding left unchanged, and the poor food with which he has been provided thrown carelessly into the refuse and offal which surround him. Clean and fastidious, as the lion always is about his food and person, he often refuses to eat, and this, added sometimes to seasickness, makes his suffering terrible.

The finest health and strength will not stand such a strain for long, and by the time the journey is ended the lion is disgusted with man and his ways. In many cases he arrives in Europe or America sick and weak, and appears only too ready to die and get rid of his troubles. The only passion he has in this state is a genuine hate for man, and this hate seems to be the only thing which arouses him at all.

It frequently happens that wild animals kill themselves in frenzies of fear during transportation. Everything in their surroundings is new and strange to them. They have lost their freedom and the fresh air; they are cramped and half stifled in close quarters, surrounded by dirt and unwholesomeness, and cannot even keep their bodies still for two seconds, owing to the perpetual motion which goes on, and which, perhaps, terrifies them more than anything else. Therefore, when a wild animal is first turned over to the trainer, he is practically mad with his experiences and terrors.

Then begins the training. One man, and one man only, has him in care, and it is always essential in these cases to choose a quiet trainer. This is one of the reasons why Captain Bonavita has made such a success in training lions. He is always quiet and self-possessed, even in times of extreme peril; and this quietness has more effect on wild animals, particularly lions, than anything else. In some way it seems to communicate itself to them and allays their fears. Often a lion rushing round and round a cage will be calmed down by a gentle "Whoa, whoa," spoken in a soothing manner.

The first thing which is done is to attend to the animal's bodily comfort. In place of dirt and unwholesomeness is cleanliness; in place of the filthy, reeking bed is a fresh, sweet one of dry straw; and fresh food and water are brought to him, always by the same trainer, who invariably speaks a few soothing words in a quiet voice when Leo begins to race wildly round the cage in the vain effort to get out. A very large cage is never given at first, but the one provided is a great improvement on his old cramped quarters. Were it too large, the animal would destroy or seriously injure himself in trying to escape. It is generally just large enough for him to turn round in comfortably, but not high enough to spring about in too much.

The feeding of the animal is the first step in his training. The trainer takes him about six pounds of fresh beef or mutton, with a piece of bone, once a day, and fresh, clear water three times a day. No one but the trainer is permitted to go near him or to look at him. He must become acquainted with the trainer's personality, and must be made to realize that his food and drink come from the trainer only. He must also be made clearly to understand that the trainer means him no harm, but does everything for his comfort.

The meat is usually put upon the end of a long iron fork, and passed to him through the bars. He has to come a little way forward to take the meat, and gradually, without thinking about it, he comes close to the trainer. At first the water-pan is tied to the edge of the cage, because in trying to draw the pan toward him the animal would upset it and make the cage wet and uncomfortable. There would also be the difficulty of getting it out again with a stick, which might arouse the animal's anger.

When the lion and his trainer have once become acquainted, he is transferred to another cage; and here again, for two weeks, he is fed, watered, and taken care of by the same trainer, until the animal not only gets accustomed to him. but looks forward to his presence, because it invariably means something pleasant to himself. In about six weeks' time a loose collar is slipped around the lion's neck when he is asleep. Attached to this collar is a chain, long enough for the animal to move about, but just short enough to keep him from reaching the end of the cage.

The next step is for the trainer to put a chair inside the cage. Instantly the lion springs for it, but, being kept in check by the chain, finds he cannot reach it, and retires to a corner, growling sulkily at the intruder. After casting vindictive glances at it, with occasional growls, he becomes accustomed to its presence and takes no further notice of it. Then the trainer, after opening the door of the cage once or twice and looking in, finally walks calmly in himself and sits on the chair. He is just out of reach of the lion, and when the animal has growled and resented it as he did the chair, he again subsides into indifference.

Then comes the time when the lion is released from the chain, when the trainer takes his life in his hands, and when he knows that the moment of extreme danger has arrived. No matter how quiet and docile the lion may have appeared to be when chained, he is likely to develop suddenly a ferocious savagery when released.

At this stage Captain Bonavita always carries two stout oak sticks, one in the right hand and one in the left. The one in the right he keeps for immediate use, and when once punished with this stick, the lion, not knowing the purpose of the stick in the left hand, comes to fear that also and backs away from it. If possible, the sticks are used to stroke the lion, if he will permit it; for the condition of a wild animal is one of receptivity—he is willing to welcome anything that will give him pleasure. But it is rarely, indeed, at this stage of the proceedings that he will allow this.

In the first place, the lion is generally a little frightened or nervous himself, and alarm begets wrath. It is feline nature to dissemble that wrath until the moment of action. Leo does not growl or lash his tail. It is not the growling lion that is to be feared

ELEPHANTS AND TRAINER

most, nor does the lashing tail, as so many suppose, indicate danger. Not anger, but good humor, comes from such indications. It is when the tail stands out straight and rigid that the trainer begins to think of retreat.

When the tail becomes stiff in this manner, it is generally a pretty sure indication that the animal is going to spring. When the trainer sees that tail become like an iron bar, he tries to slip out at the door; sometimes he knows he will never have the opportunity. Before the lion springs he glances aside carelessly, growling quietly, and the next instant, with open mouth and all four paws distended, he is sailing through the air, straight for the throat of the man, his tense body rigid with passion, and his five hundred pounds of sinew and muscle ready to descend on the intruder.

The man who will not have foreseen that terrific onslaught, holding himself in readiness for it, has no business with wild animals, and will, in all probability, never again attempt any dealings with them, because he will never have the chance. The agility which is one of the requisite qualities for a trainer must come into play, and upon it depends his life.

It is here that the chair, which plays no small part in an animal's education, comes into use again. That chair was not brought into the cage merely for comfort. It is the best defense possible against the lion's spring. Swift and apparently unpremeditated as the spring has been, the man has seen the tenseness of the muscles that preceded it, and before the animal has reached him, the stout legs of the chair are bristling between them.

Here is another problem for the lion. This unknown thing has suddenly assumed an unexpected and possibly a deadly significance. Snarling, he drops on his haunches and claws at the barrier; perhaps he has plumped into it and has felt the blows from its dull prongs. Then out from behind it springs a stick—the same stick of his pleasant memories, but turned to base uses now, for it flicks him smartly on the tip of his nose, just where a lion keeps all his most sensitive feelings.

Again it lands, and the chances are ten to one that two blows on that tender spot are enough. Howling with rage and discomfiture, the lion ceases to claw the chair and retires to his corner, very crestfallen and extremely puzzled and bewildered. By the time he has had leisure to consider the strange performance, the trainer is out of the cage, leaving the chair behind him.

Now the lion may do any one or all of several things, according to the depth of his emotions. He may glower and sulk in his corner; he may rant and tear about his cage, giving vent to his outraged feelings in loud roars; he may go for the chair and dismember it (not without scars to his own hide, probably); or he may settle down to think matters over calmly, possibly coming to the conclusion that it is unwise to attack any strange thing before finding out whether it can hurt in return.

Generally, after this chair incident, when the lion has got the worst of it, he calms down fairly soon, and on the reappearance of his trainer some time afterward has evidently forgotten the unpleasantness of it all, and remembers only that it is the trainer who brings him all he wants. In some cases he greets him

with a gentle rubbing against the bars of his
cage and a soft purr, for he is only a big cat,
after all. The meat is taken with a slightly
subdued air, he allows himself to be stroked
and patted,—outside the bars,—and so another great step in his education has been
taken and accomplished successfully.

CHAPTER IX

HOW WILD BEASTS ARE TAUGHT TRICKS

THE next stage in the training of a lion is for the trainer to enter the cage again with the chair and stick. No longer militant, but somewhat timid, the animal keeps in his corner, furtively watching the trainer. Little by little, the man edges the chair over until he is within reach; then he begins to rub the lion with his stick. Little by little he decreases the distance still more, until, finally, he has his hand on the lion's shoulder and is patting him gently.

This is another great step in advance. The lion has learned to endure the touch of the human hand; although he murmurs sulkily, he likes it, for few animals are indifferent to petting. Day by day the trainer familiarizes the lion with his presence and touch; rubbing his back, stroking his shoulders, raising his paws,—a somewhat risky and ticklish trial,—and in the course of about two weeks after first entering the cage, if the animal be of fairly good temper, all alarm and overt enmity have been eradicated, so accustomed has the animal become to the presence of this one man.

After this he is taught to back until he reaches the rear of the cage, and then made to lie down. After a time he is made to lie down and stand up, at either the word of command or at a certain cue, and after each act of obedience he is given a small piece of raw meat as a reward. If he does not obey, he gets no reward, and in time the habit becomes strong, and he does what is required of him, whether he gets anything for it or not.

Then comes another period of extreme danger for the trainer. This is when the animal first enters the arena. He finds himself in a place which seems vast after a cage, and becoming a little bewildered at the strange surroundings, behaves in an entirely different manner. Many animals who have been taught to perform in comparatively small cages have to be trained all over again when in the arena. In the big arena, therefore, the training of the animals has to be practically begun anew.

This is one reason why trainers are always so anxious to get their animals out of the training-schools and -cages and into the arena as soon as possible. But they are liable to get them there too soon sometimes, which is extremely dangerous. I have already explained why a lion is first put into a small cage to begin with. If he goes into the arena too soon, he is more apt to spring at the trainer, because he has not yet become tractable and docile enough.

On first entering the arena, the lion runs round and round, seeking some place to escape, because his surroundings are strange. He is also rather frightened, for anything unusual or strange always makes a wild animal, especially a lion, nervous; but the trainer's quiet presence and voice generally soothe him after a while, and he soon gets used to it. An entire day is generally taken to accustom the lion to his new surroundings, and he is then put through several evolutions, just as in the smaller cage.

Beginning at this point, the training or education of an animal is simply the application to more advanced work of the principles already followed. It is progress beyond a kind of kindergarten, and learning by association has everything to do with it. The animal is becoming amenable to the mastery of man, and in doing so his own reason is being developed. From this time on he begins to take a new interest in life. That instinct of action, which he has inherited from his ancestors and which has been slumbering, is awakened, and he is learning to know and enjoy the cultivated exercise.

He works gradually into the harness, and soon becomes an adept at the work which he has been taught with so much painstaking patience. But he always remains an animal, his natural instincts are always paramount, and though he may go through his performances meekly, and even with a certain amount of interest, there are always deep down in him an inborn distrust and fear of man.

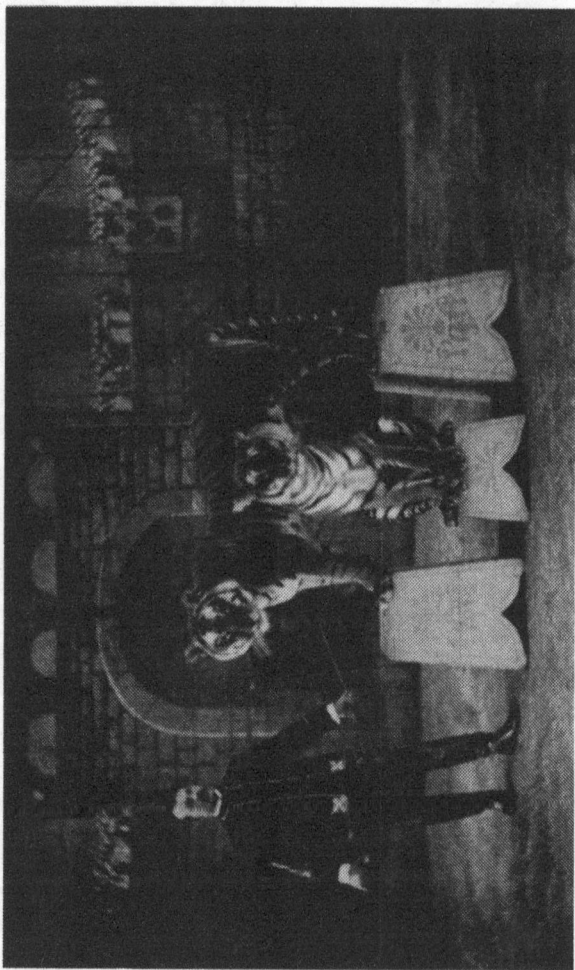

TRAINED BUT NOT TAMED

The only trainer, therefore, who has any business in a cage with such animals is one who thoroughly understands their nature, who knows all their weaknesses and characteristics, and who fears their strength. If I ever hear a trainer make a remark to the effect that, after all, there is nothing to be afraid of when once an animal is trained, I know that man is unfit to be a trainer at all. The man who makes the best trainer is the one who realizes their treachery, and knows that there is danger at all times and in all places with wild animals, no matter how well trained they may be. As I said before, no wild animal is ever tamed, only trained, and the best training in the world is nothing when once the animal feels inclined to give way to his natural savage instincts.

In time, the trained animal becomes so accustomed to performing, that when he sees the paraphernalia of his performance he knows exactly what is expected of him, and does it naturally and readily. The successful performance of all trained animals depends on this almost instinctive following of long-

8

accustomed habit, together with the pleasure the exercise gives to animals habitually confined in small cages.

Leopards, panthers, and jaguars are all trained in much the same manner. Mme. Morelli puts them through a course of training very similar to that given the lion. They are taught to respect and look for the trainer, and have instilled into them as much awe as is ever bred in any animal, which is not saying a great deal. The jaguar, leopard, and panther become used to the association of the trainer, and are finally willing, through much coaxing and coercion, to perform such elementary feats as are required of them.

The stick is the instrument for the education of these animals in the same manner as in the case of the lion. To begin with, a broomstick is laid on the floor, and the trainer steps to the back of the stage, apparently unarmed, leaving the stick in full sight, the animal crouching in the rear of the cage. After a few moments' hesitation, with the tense, strained tightening of his leg-muscles,— which all trainers know so well as a signal of danger,—the animal launches its sleek, compact, sinewy body full upon the unprotected broomstick.

The dull wood, like a craven, has not spunk enough to respond. It accepts the punishment as a Chinaman does in battle, with no apparent expectation of anything different. The animal, disgusted, leaves the stick and launches himself at the trainer. The trainer, small and delicate woman as she is, meets the charge with coolness and that quiet reserve force which stands all trainers in such good stead. The broomstick is not her only weapon. She has another: an iron prong, heavy, thick, and with a point dull enough to leave whatever skin it touches unlacerated, but sharp enough to remind any animal that he is in poor business in an attack on it, when held in the hands of a determined trainer.

The prong is attached to the end of a stick much larger and longer than the first stick, and against that combination the animal throws himself. He comes out of the encounter with a cowed air and an added respect for the small woman who held it. He slinks again into his corner, but allows himself to be finally coaxed out and stroked with the very stick which had resisted his first spring in such a decided manner.

Finally, the stick is laid on the floor, and after much persuasion, the animal is induced to walk over it, which he does, hissing and snarling. He is led over it again and again, and fails to notice that each time the stick is raised a little from the floor, until finally he finds, somewhat to his surprise and discomfiture, that when he walks over the stick he has to make quite a spring in order to get over it at all. Before this stick incident is finished, he jumps over a stick raised as high as a chair.

No animal is ever allowed to backslide. Each thing done one day must be done the next day in exactly the same way; there must be no deviation from the rule. This is the reason that in every animal act the trainer positively insists upon perfect adherence to the regular formula. Such is the force of habit that laxity to-day means a desire for laxity to-morrow at the same place and in the same way, and laxity in one small detail will

"DEPEW"

breed the tendency for it, which will then in all probability spread and in a short time affect the whole performance. This is why everything is done with such careful attention to detail.

If an animal is sent to the right side on entering the arena the first day, he is sent to the right every day thereafter, and the direction in which he goes after leaving his pedestal, and before taking his place in the group, is always the same. Each animal, too, in a group has his own place and his own time for assuming the place; and should he once leave it, there would be danger to the whole performance. The trainer, too, even in walking about the arena, always walks in the same way, and gives his closest attention to the prevention of the happening of anything unusual.

Performing animals particularly dislike a change in the stage setting, and it is absolutely necessary, whenever a new one is contemplated, to accustom them to it by the most gradual means. There have been times when an animal, seeing a new barrel or block for the first time, would attack it with such gusto that not only would the objectionable piece of furniture be destroyed, but so much excitement would be communicated to the other animals that it would be found impossible to go on with the act.

The dangerous tigress, Goldie, which performs with Herman Weedon, has a special dislike to the red pedestal on which she has to sit during the performance. At all other times, when this pedestal is out of sight, Goldie is as meek and mild as a kitten, and will allow herself to be smoothed and stroked with every symptom of pleasure. But when once that red pedestal is in view, Goldie is a fury. At one time Herman Weedon tried painting the objectionable stool another color, but he soon found that in Goldie's case it was not the color or the pedestal itself that she objected to: it was the fact that when she saw that pedestal she knew that she had to perform, which raised all her temper and animosity.

An incident which occurred in Kansas City will well illustrate the force of habit in wild animals. An error on the part of the workmen had caused Mme. Pianka's cage to be misplaced, and it became necessary that a smaller one be substituted. Such a change from one accustomed condition to another is one which performing animals particularly dislike, and it is avoided whenever possible, but in this case it was unavoidable.

The lions all objected to the change, and showed their displeasure by many unmistakable signs. One lioness absolutely refused to enter the cage at all; Mme. Pianka coaxed, ordered, and flicked her whip. The lioness had been a good animal, but some unaccountable sulkiness, such as is likely to obtrude into the good nature of any animal at any time, had taken possession of her, and nothing would move her.

It was at this juncture that I decided to enter her cage myself and insist on obedience. The lioness looked casually at me and then at the small riding-whip in my hand, and after a little demur went into the cage and through her act without any more fuss or sulkiness. I was in the act of leaving the cage when I, thoughtlessly, did a most foolish thing.

Pleased to think I had subdued the big cat, I carelessly tapped the riding-whip on the ground, merely for a flourish. Twenty feet away the lioness's mate was standing, watching the whole proceeding with dubious eyes. He promptly noted the action, had never seen it before, mistook its intent for an attack on his mate, and with a single bound was on me. Before I had time to realize what was happening, the lion had pinned me through the fleshy part of the thigh, and we both went down together.

The lion loosened his hold, gathered himself up, and picking me up in his mouth, as though I were a tiny child, carried me over to Pianka, as though for her approval. Here, fortunately for myself, the force of habit again came into play.

In Mme. Pianka's hand was the revolver, loaded with blank cartridges, which she used for her act. Two of these she fired, in quick succession, close to the lion's ear. That was one of the signals for a change in his act; the other, a simultaneous one, was to throw her arm about his neck. The natural pose which had always been suggested by these two actions in conjunction worked the charm. The force of habit brought him to instant obedience, he drew his teeth out of my body, fell into the pose, and seemed quite oblivious of the anger that had only the moment before aroused him to his dangerous attack.

I scrambled to my feet, and after running the lion once or twice round the arena, just to demonstrate that I still had the mastery, went off to bed. The teeth had not touched the bone, but there were some bad flesh wounds, and I was not up again for three weeks. And all this was through a foolish little bit of byplay to which the lion was not accustomed.

After the animal has learned his lesson and become expert in his performance, there still remains the test of a public appearance. This is always a matter of anxiety for the trainer, as animals suffer from stage fright. The sight of a crowd is likely to distract them and draw their attention from the trainer, so that they lose their cues. Once thoroughly accustomed to the stage, they seem to find in it a sort of intoxication well known to a species higher in the order of nature. Nearly all trainers assert that animals are affected by the attitude of an audience, that they are stimulated by the applause of an enthusiastic house, and perform indifferently before a cold audience.

The pleasure in acting and showing off before others is, perhaps, more plainly demonstrated by bears than by any other animals. The conceit and good opinion of themselves which some performing bears have is absolutely ridiculous. One trainer, Roberto, has cleverly trained some very young bears to perform various acts. The duty of one is to climb up a ladder, set free the American flag, and sit on the top of the ladder until his trainer has played a tune on the violin while he balances the bear on the ladder.

So proud is the little bear of his accomplishment that whenever any one is looking on, he will go through the whole performance by himself, evidently simply for the pleasure of doing it, and no one can fail to see the conceitedness of his manner as he does it. Bears very seldom get nervous in public; they enjoy the acts too much.

More animals are lost to the arena from fear than through viciousness. Trainers dread a timid lion, tiger, or leopard, not only because in its panic it is likely to injure the trainer, but because it is unreliable, and may take fright and spoil a whole performance. When animals are found to be so unusually timid that it is impossible to rely on them, they are not used for any of the higher classes of performances, but are employed for the more simple sensational acts, which often take the public quite as much as the more difficult feats, but which require little preparatory education.

In cases of wild animals in captivity suddenly seizing a keeper or other person, the best means to make them loosen their hold is either to fire off blank cartridges or to turn a hose on them. Generally the hose has the greatest effect, as it stops the animal's breath for the time, and he loosens his hold to breathe. In many cases, however, nothing in the world will induce a wild animal to loosen his hold.

and in this case it is merely a matter of brute strength, which it is impossible to overcome, except by killing the animal, and even then he will often hold on long enough to finish his victim.

The keeping of red-hot irons in case of emergencies I discarded about ten or eleven years ago. I rejected it because it is an extremely cruel expedient, and seldom effectual as a remedy for the attacks of wild beasts. This fact was contradicted a short time ago by a man who stated that he saw some irons being heated in one of the coke fires. So he did, but this was in the winter, and my practice is then to put hot irons into the drinking-water of the animals occasionally. This practice is always observed in all my shows during the winter months. It has the value of taking the chill off the water, and also imparts some of the beneficial qualities of the iron, thus giving an iron tonic and drinkable water at the same time.

For the reason that it is cruel and unsafe, I never now allow any firearms to be used, unless it is in a case of great urgency. I took this

A DIFFICULT FEAT

precaution after an incident in Chicago, when
the cheek of a spectator was grazed by a shot
fired by a trainer at one of his infuriated animals. The weapons that are used now are
intelligence, pluck, vigilance, and patience.
With these used in the proper way, very few
animals in captivity, whether trained or not,
will do those about them any harm.

CHAPTER X

AN ANIMAL SHOW AT NIGHT

TO those who are the least timid or not accustomed to it, an animal show at night has a gruesome and somewhat terrifying aspect.

The general impression is, that when the trainer has made his final bow and the band has given a gentle suggestion to those departing by playing "Say 'Au revoir,' and not good-by," everything is over and finished for the day.

But to the chief trainers, the day—or night—is only just beginning. For it is at night, when the majority of people are in bed and asleep, that the principal work of animal training begins. There are various reasons for this.

All carnivora are nocturnal animals, and

although after many years in captivity they
get into the habit of sleeping part of the night,
they are generally more or less alert and
wakeful.   During the day they are lazy,
sleepy, and somewhat stupid, but as night
draws near they begin to be restless, and it
has been found far less difficult to attract their
attention in the night time than either in the
early morning or during the day.

Also, there are no workers or loiterers
round the place to take off their attention
when being taught new tricks,—the least
thing will attract an animal's attention,—and
there are also more time and opportunity for
arranging the hoists, or cranes, with which
some animals are taught to understand what
is wanted of them.   These are used chiefly for
teaching elephants to stand on their hind legs,
to lift up a fore leg and walk on the remain-
ing three, or to lie down.

In teaching him to stand up on his hind legs,
the ropes are attached to each of his fore legs,
and at certain words of command they are
gently hoisted into the air, leaving the elephant supporting himself on his hind legs.

This has to be done sometimes as often as fifteen or sixteen times before he understands what he is wanted to do, but after a while, simply from force of habit, he begins to raise himself at the signal, and although the ropes are still kept round his legs, he will gradually get into the way of doing the whole thing himself, seemingly unconsciously.

Much the same sort of thing is done in teaching him to lie down, only in this case a rope with a slip noose is passed round his body at the small of his back, one hind foot and one fore foot are tied and moved out from under him, and then the ropes are pulled gently but firmly until he lies down. When this has been done six or eight times, the elephant generally lies down of his own accord.

Not only does it take some time to arrange the cranes, but, as it needs sometimes eight or ten men to help, these men are told off for certain nights for an hour or so's work, and are able then to give their undivided attention to what they are doing. For elephants, although most intelligent animals when trained, are sometimes extremely difficult to teach,

"DOC" BALANCING HIMSELF ON A BALL PLACED ON A SEE-SAW

while their great bulk and strength make them formidable creatures to annoy.

One of the first things an elephant is taught to do is to walk round the arena without running away. Some elephants show in the earliest stage of training that they can never be persuaded not to bolt at every opportunity, and this is another reason why so much of the training takes place at night. Should an elephant take it into his head to stop suddenly and go out, he would follow out his intention at the risk of danger and death to those not only inside the show, but outside.

Were he to do this in the daytime, the chances are that he would cause a panic, but at night the darkness and quiet have a soothing effect upon him, and even supposing he should get out,—which rarely occurs, as great precautions are taken,—there are few people abroad for him to injure. Even a well-trained elephant will sometimes stop his tricks abruptly and calmly walk out of the arena. In this case, however, there is no danger whatever, as he simply wants to go back to his house and eat peanuts and biscuits, as he

9

was doing when interrupted for the performance.

To make an elephant stand on a barrel or cylinder is simply a matter of inducing him to remain there. Ten chances to one he will bolt in the middle of it; but there is no need to teach him to balance himself—he will attend to that himself. The same applies to see-sawing: he begins with a plank, and gradually gets accustomed to the movement. These methods are simple, but many months, expended in short and frequent lessons delivered with great patience, must be consumed in instruction in order to make a success of it.

Quiet and brevity are important considerations in the lessons. What is to us no appreciable exertion requires an effort on the part of an animal which soon wearies it, and, if care is not taken, disgusts it, and this makes it incapable of further instruction until it has rested. There is also the danger that if too much instruction is given at a time, or if strangers are present, the animal will not only be irritated but rebellious, and finally refuse to do anything at all. There is then nothing to be done but to give up the idea of ever making a performer of the animal, and let him be a mere figure in the show.

It will thus be seen how essential it is to do the chief part of the training by night. There is only one runway behind the cages, and no one is ever allowed in the training-school or in the runway during a performance; and as no performance is given after eleven, the trainers can rest assured that there is no danger of an accidental meeting. In this way all risk of two trainers and their animals meeting in the runway is avoided.

Therefore, as soon as the public has disappeared after the evening performance, a busy time begins in the animal-show. Most of the lights are turned out. The bolts, bars, and doors of each cage are looked at; certain men go round the show at stated intervals to make sure that there is no danger of fire, and the trainers equip themselves for their dangerous experiments, and begin to turn their animals out for their lessons.

By this time most of the animals have partly settled down for the night, with the exception of some few who, unable to forget their natural feelings, are restlessly pacing up and down their cages. But however quiet it may happen to be at the time of closing, the minute a trainer makes his animals come out of their various cages and go into the arena, peace is at an end. To get the animals out of their cages and into the arena is most difficult and dangerous. Sometimes they come out with a rush at the trainer and his assistants, and sometimes they remain in a corner and refuse to move in spite of persuasions, coaxings, or threats. In this case there is nothing for the trainer to do but to go into the cage and drive the animal out.

The animal generally gives in, and finally leaves the cage and sulkily betakes himself to the arena; but he always relieves his feelings by growls or roars, and these resentful protests are promptly answered by nearly all the other animals in the building.

This is specially the case when a strange animal is led out, for animals are peculiarly quick in recognizing and resenting the presence of a stranger. The natural instinct is

to get at the intruder and have a fight, in order to prove which is the superior of the two,
and, failing in this, their only form of relief
lies in roaring at the top of their voices.
When one starts, another follows, and then
another, until at last scarcely an animal in the
building is silent.

The lion generally starts with three big
roars, ending up with the curious, short, gasp-
ing barks so characteristic of him.   The other
lions follow in chorus; the tigers roar in concert; the jaguars, leopards, and panthers give
their peculiar coughing growls; the peccary
sends forth his choking cry, so like a desperate
appeal for help; and the bears growl a surly
accompaniment.

Occasionally, should an elephant be receiving his first lessons, he will introduce a few
notes of shrill trumpeting as a relief to the
roars and growls, and a hyena will suddenly
burst out in fiendish, hysterical laughter,
while the wolves and coyotes keep up a low,
monotonous howling, which to some people is
worse than all the other cries, screams, and
roars put together.

Added to all these weird sounds, the cages, with the exception of the arena, are in darkness, and the soft, stealthy tread of footsteps and an occasional gleam of green and yellow eyes from all corners, make it necessary that trainers should not only have strong muscles and nerves, but plenty of cool courage and self-control. For many of the strongest men are totally unnerved by surroundings of this kind.

There is, of course, always the chance that an animal *may* get out, and if a man once begins to dwell on these things and becomes nervous, imagining he hears various noises, his training is absolutely worthless. He must give his whole, undivided attention to what he is doing, both for his own sake and that of the animal he is training.

Of course, accidents occur while training as well as when performing in public, but comparatively few accidents ever take place at night. This may possibly be because there is nothing likely to startle the animals, or because they themselves feel the effect of the dim lights and the silence.

A curious thing once happened which might have proved disastrous. A trainer had been through his performance with his animals, had seen them safely back into their cages, and was just going through the building on his way to his rooms, which were overhead, when he thought he heard a movement. It sounded like the scuttling of a rat, and, being unable to see what it was, he struck a match and lighted a small lantern he carried in his hand.

He was shutting the little door of the lantern leisurely (for the greatest precautions have to be observed in case of fire), when something rubbed against him softly. Thinking it was his dog come to look for him, he put his hand down to stroke him, and then found he was stroking the back of a lion! The animal appeared to be dazed by the sudden flash of the lantern thrown in his eyes, and the trainer speaking quietly to the other men who were settling matters up for the night, the king of beasts was persuaded to return to his cage close by before he had time to recover from his astonishment.

It was entirely due to the prompt presence of mind of this trainer that no harm came from this incident; for as soon as the door was closed on the lion, he appeared to realize that he had lost a good opportunity, and did his best to get out again, but it was too late. It was found that a bolt had loosened in its socket, and when the animal had rubbed against the door, it had fallen out and freed him.

In using the arena at night for training, the trainers generally arrange among themselves as to what time, and for how long, each man shall have it. In this way, all the trainers get a certain time without clashing with one another, and it can be readily seen that where there are several trainers, the training sometimes goes on all night long.

Whether this happens or not, the animals, one and all, indulge in a general chorus at daybreak. This is, perhaps, even more weird than the combined noises in the night, for the dim morning light makes the building full of shadows, and each cage is full of restless animals pacing to and fro. As the light gets

JAGUARS, LEOPARDS, AND PANTHERS

stronger they settle down again, though first one large head and then another will be lifted at the sound of the men who first come in to clean up either whistling or speaking to one another.

After this they are fairly still, until they are roused while their cages are cleaned and washed out; then each trainer goes round and attends to his own animals, and after that comes feeding-time. The carnivora are given their pieces of meat; the other animals have what is best suited to them; and many other things are done until the public once more appears to witness another performance.

CHAPTER XI

THE PRINCIPLES OF TRAINING

IT is a long time since naturalists and philosophers maintained the doctrine that animals, being controlled by instinct, were quite incapable of comprehending new ideas, and of acquiring and memorizing novel things which they have been taught to do by man.

Many reflective men now believe that the mind of an animal differs from the human intellect only in degree. The extent of this difference, however, remains a question, and one on which close observation of domestic animals, and more particularly of wild animals trained for public amusement, is calculated to throw a great deal of light.

Through a study of wild animals in their native haunts there may be learned what progress each has made in adapting itself to

the natural conditions of its life; but the study
of trained animals, placed under new conditions and influences, will show whether these
are capable of further or, at any rate, diver-
gent advancement intellectually, and give
some hint of the probable limit of this progress. It may then be seen to what extent the
animal trainer has gone in his development of
brute intellect, and that that development has
come about under conditions not entirely dis-
similar to those observed in the advancement
of the intellect of the higher species of
animals.

It should be noted, first, that "taming" and
" training " are two different words express-
ing two distinct ideas. " Taming " is merely
inducing an animal to abandon its natural
fierce disposition so far as to come under human control and be more or less sociable
with man. It is a matter in which animals
differ very widely, not only as between classes,
but as between individuals of the same species.

Moreover, tameness seems to be a matter of
the disposition rather than of the intellect,
and, perhaps, pertains to a lower rather than

to a higher grade of intelligence, for it is noticeable that some of the animals most apt in the school of the trainer abandon only slightly, if at all, their native savagery. On the other hand, some animals thoroughly domesticated seem quite incapable of any degree of education, though this may be from the fact that no one has tried it in a continuous or systematic way.

It would be hazardous to say that any animal organism is too low to manifest, had we eyes to see it, some intelligence superior to instinct. It is said that even fishes can be taught simple actions, although personally I have had no proof of it. Serpents can also be taught a little, though performing snakes are usually simply submitting to be put through certain motions in the hands of their keepers. But from birds up to elephants, the most intelligent of all animals, there is not one species, it may safely be said, which is not more or less amenable to the training of man.

It is a delusion to think that a wild animal is ever really " tamed." He acquires, through passiveness and receptivity, an amenity to man's control, and for the time being drops his ferocity. This is partly because of the inducements which are placed in his way. He has all that an animal can want,—food, cleanliness, indolence, proper exercise, even affection,—everything but freedom, but he only bows to man's will because man, through the exercise of his intelligence, takes advantage of the animal's ignorance. Every animal trainer thoroughly understands what the public does not know—that the trained animal is a product of science; but the tamed animal is a chimera of the optimistic imagination, a forecast of the millennium.

The first principle that is taught a trainer is: "Never let an animal know his power." The moment he realizes that, he is likely to use his terrible teeth, or still more terrible claws, for I always try to impress upon the trainers that each animal is, as it were, possessed of five mouths, as he can do as much, if not more, damage with each of his four feet as with his mouth.

The very moment an animal realizes his power, his training is at an end. He grows insolent, and in nine cases out of ten proceeds to wreak his vengeance on the trainer for what he concludes are past outrages; his fear has gone, and with his knowledge comes power, and his animal ferocity, long slumbering and awaiting an opening, breaks out with re-doubled vigor. The only thing to be done is for the trainer to get out as soon as possible, and let that particular animal lead a solitary life for the remainder of his days.

This is one of the reasons that everything is done to further the animal's increased respect for mankind. If he makes a scratch on a trainer, the man does not resent it in any way, for he does not wish the animal to know that he is capable of inflicting injury. Should the animal become aware in the slightest degree that what has been done is an evidence of any superior ability, he might naturally presume upon it and proceed to hurt the trainer in some other manner.

Many animals do, of course, inflict injuries upon the trainers fairly often, but it is a most unwise trainer who ever makes the slightest sign of pain or annoyance. Trainers have been known to give a flick of the whip, or some other punishment, but the result is always the same. Either the animal promptly retorts in some real injury, or indulges in a fit of the sulks which he is slow to forget. The blow he, as a rule, never forgets.

Not long ago, Herman Weedon went to greet his favorite bear, Doc, in the early morning. It is his custom to put his face close to the bear for a morning kiss or caress, to which the bear responds affectionately. In this case, Herman was outside the cage, and the bear, wishing to get his face closer, put out one paw to draw it nearer. The long claws tore the flesh of the trainer's face, and injured his eye so badly that it was feared he would lose his sight. But no punishment was given to the animal, neither was he allowed to know what he had done or to what extent his terrible claws had hurt the trainer. The animal had intended no harm, and it would have been most unwise to let him know how easily he could hurt, so no notice whatever was taken of the matter.

There are many slight attacks made by animals such as that in which Young Wallace tore my leg. This was simply an accident, and not intentional on the part of the animal, therefore it did not go against his character. No performer is put on the list of bad animals unless he makes a direct and full attack. Striking at the trainer with the paws may amount to very little; it may be purely accidental. It is the spring that counts. Every trainer expects to be clawed somewhat, and there is no successful trainer who has remained in the business long enough to entitle him to the name of trainer, and does not bear many marks of scratches and tears somewhere on his body.

My own body and limbs are elaborately tattooed with testimonials from my feline friends of many years past, for from my earliest boyhood I have been in intimate contact with the carnivora in the menagerie. All this is a matter of course.

The beast that springs, however, must either be cowed into submission quickly, or the trainer must escape from the cage as soon as possible. If the animal really means busi-

EXCHANGING CONFIDENCES

ness, it is the man's part and duty to get out, for no man can stand against the strength of a lion, the cautious spring of a tiger, or the tremendous power and terrible agility of a leopard or jaguar.

Supposing a man gets fairly cornered, the best defense against a charging lion or tiger is to strike the animal on the nose, hitting up from under; but this is by no means an easy thing to do, as the animal will spring and dodge with a degree of skill that would do credit to a master of the prize ring. Meantime, however, the man can have been edging into a position that will give him an opportunity to escape.

The felines—lions, tigers, jaguars, and leopards—jump for the throat. That is the objective point against which all carnivora make their most decided attack. It is in this way that they hunt their jungle prey, and they carry the practices of the jungle into their association with human beings. An agile man, —and no man should be allowed to become an animal trainer if he is not agile,—when he sees that the animal is going to leap,

10

can avoid the onset and get in a blow that will not injure the animal, but will send him cringing to the other end of the cage.

It is when knocked down that the great danger comes to the trainer. On his feet he is the master, but for prostrate humanity an animal has no respect whatever. On his feet there is always a chance of controlling the animals; but when down his power is gone. The minute his body touches the floor the man ceases to be master. If knocked down, the man's only chance is to struggle to the bars and raise himself, for back on his feet he may stem the tide of onslaught. A stick, a whip, a chair, perseverance, and aggressive pluck will then be his weapons of subjugation.

Some animals train easily; others learn their lessons with great diffidence and some reluctance. What one lion may learn in a week may take another a month; what one tiger may do in two lessons may take another one several months even to imitate feebly. One may as well try to give a hard and set rule for the rearing of a child, taking it through nursing, kindergarten, the primary grade, the high school and into college, without allowing the slightest leeway for the personal equation, as to say what is necessary for the training of an animal in general. Each is a study, alone and complete in itself, and each animal has its distinct individuality.

One of the greatest factors in training is to secure prompt obedience from the animals, not only at the beginning, but always. When once an animal is taught to go to a certain place, the next thing is to make him clearly understand that he is to stay there until he has his cue to come down again. This is important in more ways than one.

In the first place, the fact of their staying on their pedestals means everything to the trainer—probably his life. When once the animals have been made to know that they must not get down until told, the trainer is safe. Very few, if any, beasts will spring from a pedestal. It is an awkward place to spring from, for one thing, and there is not room to give enough impetus, for another. But when an animal is on the ground, there is never any knowing what he may take into his head to do next.

There is absolutely no danger to the woman trainer, La Belle Selica, no matter how much she dances and pirouettes in front of and around her lions, as long as they keep on their pedestals. It is when one gets down that the danger threatens. Then there is not only the probability that the lion will spring, but there is also the chance, and a very great one, that all the other lions will also get down, for what one animal does another generally does too. This trainer was attacked at one time in this very manner.

She had entered the arena, got all four lions up on their pedestals, and was half way through her dance, when one lioness got slowly and indifferently down and settled herself comfortably on the floor. This would not do; so, still going on with her dancing, the trainer ordered the lioness up again. Not feeling inclined to get up, the lioness growled a little, in return for which La Belle Selica flicked her with a small whip that she carried in her hand. Unfortunately, at this mo-

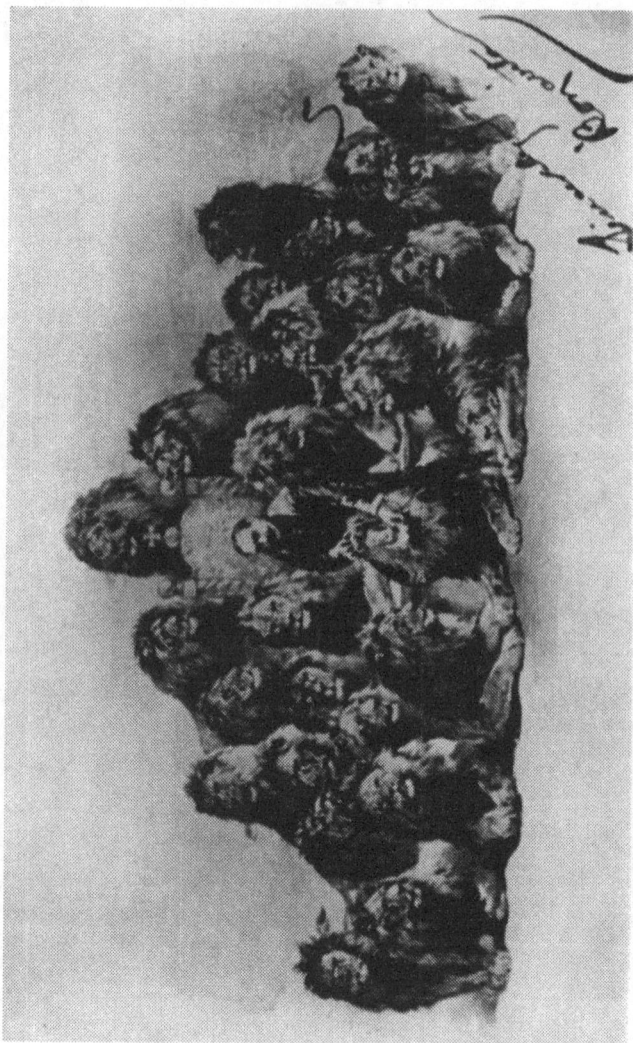

THE LARGEST NUMBER OF LIONS EVER GROUPED

ment another lion got down, and the trainer not only had the lioness to tackle, but had also to keep a sharp lookout for the other lion.

She gave another flick with her whip, but at another growl from the lioness the second lion sprang forward and knocked the trainer down. In a wonderful manner she was up again in a moment, and the lion's attention being attracted from outside the arena by two of the trainers, La Belle Selica was able to get out without much injury. By the time she reached the door both the other lions had also got down, and it is doubtful whether she would not have lost her life had she not been very quick. The curious thing was that at her next performance the lions seemed to have forgotten all about the incident, and were perfectly obedient, none seeming to have any wish to get down at all.

One of the most dangerous moments in the whole of Captain Bonavita's performance is when he first enters and has to get all twenty-seven lions up on the pedestals. Dozens of things may happen before he gets them there. A lion may be in a playful mood and catch him by the leg, throwing him down; one of them may get in his way and trip him up; he may get a blow from one of the many hard, ropy tails, or a pat from one of the huge paws. One or two lions may suddenly consider that this would be a good time to spring on him; a couple of them may have a romp together, and so knock against him; and, what is far more serious, one or two may begin a quarrel which may end in a free fight, in which all the others would be only too ready to join.

All these things may happen before he is able to get them on the pedestals; but, when once there, the force of habit and obedience has become so strong, and the personal influence of this trainer is so powerful, that it is an exceedingly rare thing for even one of the twenty-seven to once get down. Occasionally this will happen, but a steady look from Bonavita, a motion from his whip, and the lion gets slowly up from the floor, ascends the pedestal, and puts on an indifferent air, as though he had been there all the time.

Absolute obedience from the animals is one of the great foundations of training. Without it, there would be no performing animals, and no trainer. I have seen trainers spend hours, and sometimes a whole day, insisting on an animal doing some little thing which he is reluctant to do. The thing itself, perhaps, is not very important; it may not be used in the performance at all, but it is a matter of obedience, and it must be insisted upon, no matter at what trouble or cost.

Richard De Kenzo, one of the most daring trainers, nearly lost his life at one time because he had not insisted on an animal promptly obeying him. De Kenzo prefers to train only the more savage and treacherous beasts, but in this case he had concluded that the animal was not feeling very well, and it is a strict rule that no animal who is the least sick is ever allowed to perform or be trained. For this reason, then, the animal was let off; but the next time he absolutely refused to do what was wanted of him, and the fact of trying to make him do so brought about an attack which might have ended very seriously. As it was, De Kenzo got off with a badly torn hand and arm. and was ill for several weeks.

Much has been said, and much more doubt-less imagined, by the casual observer about the control which a trainer has over his charges by reason of some magnetic power in his eye. No greater fallacy ever existed. A study of Bonavita's performance would satisfy any one as to that question. He has twenty-seven lions in the arena at one time, and is con-stantly turning his back on most of them, walking about among them, and singling out, from time to time, here and there, some one for special acts and tricks. He would require twenty-seven pairs of eyes to control his act if the eye supposition were correct.

It is not the eye,—though that may express the qualities of resoluteness, of wariness, and of patience,—it is the brain that controls a score and more of beasts like that. In associa-tion with animals of the feline species, there is an ever present element of danger, no matter how well trained they may be. Every time a trainer turns his back in a cage he risks his life: not a great risk, to be sure, but there is always a chance of death in a stroke. Yet it is impossible to keep the eye on half a dozen animals at once, let alone twenty-seven, and the man must trust to the good temper of his subjects and his own control and good fortune.

Many animals—this is true especially of lions—leap at the bars of a cage in a frenzy of rage the moment a trainer leaves them, as though furious that they had let him out alive, yet the next time he enters they are none the less completely under his dominion. So excellent is the effect of this fury on the thrill-demanding public, that some lions have been trained to do this very trick. But it is an extremely dangerous one, and one which no sensible trainer would dream of teaching his animals.

CHAPTER XII

THE ANIMAL TRAINER—SOME FAMOUS TRAINERS

TO secure the right man for the training of wild animals is about the most serious problem that the proprietor of an animal exhibition has to solve; very often the problem remains unsolved.

An animal trainer is a complex and unique person in more ways than one. He is not always superlatively endowed with the characteristics that are attributed to him by most casual observers. Curiously enough, the very element that would seem the most essential is scarcely ever reckoned as his chief virtue. Courage is considered by those who know little about it as one of the first requisites, but a man may have physical and moral courage to an unusual degree and still be quite unfit for a trainer.

The animal trainer may have, and all do have to some extent, the physical courage which is admired, but it is an unconscious courage, and plays such a minor part in a successful performance, that the possession of it is not noted, either by the trainer himself, or by those who know him. There are faculties far higher and far more difficult of cultivation, as well as more rarely possessed, which the animal trainer must have.

First of all are good personal habits. The finest lion-trainers are men of the most absolute personal integrity, who smoke and drink very little, if at all, and who possess self-control to an unusual degree. It is a fact very little known and somewhat difficult to realize by those who have not studied the matter, that in some curious, incomprehensible way, wild animals know instinctively whether men are addicted to bad habits. It is one of the many problems which are beyond the human understanding. For those who are the least bit inclined to drink, or live a loose life, the wild animal has neither fear nor respect.

He despises them with all the contempt of

his animal nature, and recognizes neither their authority nor superiority. Just as men recognize superior minds and strong personalities in other men, so does the wild animal recognize such qualities, and it is wonderful how extremely susceptible animals are to graceful, refined, and pleasing personalities.

The personality of an animal trainer is one that counts both with the animals and with the audience, and the more magnetic, polished, and accomplished he is, the greater will be his success and the stronger will be his influence, both with the animals with which he comes in contact and with the public which observes him. But if a man has begun to take just a little, or has deviated somewhat from the straight road, the animals will discover it long before his fellow-men.

From that moment the trainer's life is in danger every time he enters the cage, and the animals keep a keen lookout for the moment when he will either trip a little,—always the signal for animals to spring,—lose his nerve, or let his thoughts go wandering off to other matters, even for a moment or two. The least

HERMAN WEEDON DEFYING HIS FIERCEST LION

carelessness, the least indifference, even a little unusual movement on his part, is quite enough to make the animals spring upon him and get him down.

Occasionally a trainer who is beginning to take to drink or other bad habits realizes that he will soon lose the respect and control of his animals, and is wise enough to drop the training business before too late. But, as a rule, once a man has taken up this profession he is extremely loath to resign, although he may be perfectly well aware that he endangers his life every moment he trusts himself among the animals. There is a peculiar fascination about the life which keeps him at it; and although I have often warned men, they have rarely been induced to give it up until some severe accident has happened which has either disabled them, or given them such a shock that they lost their nerve entirely.

One of the finest lion-trainers that America ever had has now voluntarily retired, though still in the prime of life; but he is addicted to drink, realized the danger, and so was sensible enough to give it up before too late. He felt it was absolutely unsafe for him to enter the arena night after night, when no matter how little he drank had a numbing effect upon him.

The climax came one night when, feeling a little more numb than usual, he suddenly noticed in the midst of the performance that his lions were all looking at him curiously. Instantly he knew that they had lost their respect for him, for all trainers can tell, before anything happens, when the moment has come in which they are likely to lose their dominance, if that loss comes, not through accident, but through the paralysis of their own power. He realized at once the pitiful state he was drifting into, and the danger, and was wise and quick enough to get out before they got him.

But that was the last time he ever entered the cage. From being tractable and docile, the lions from that time had nothing but hatred and contempt for him, and his approach even near their cages was always the signal for savage snarls and vicious leaps at the bars.

Another essential in animal training is patience. It must be an ingrained attribute of the character, and dominant at all times—a constant, persistent, unwearying patience. Without it the trainer will never make a complete success. Allied with patience must be good judgment, and one who is patient generally has good judgment. This is one of the reasons that, as a rule, Englishmen and Germans, being more phlegmatic, make excellent animal trainers.

Trainers whose patience is limited never last long. There comes a day when, through hasty temper or a sudden loss of patience, the trainer says or does some foolish thing, which he always has reason to regret, and bitterly, too.

In one case, one of the animals would not respond to his cue, in spite of being spoken to several times. The trainer kept his patience for some time, but the fact that the audience was getting restless made him nervous, and in a foolish moment he shouted at the lion. The shout was so unusual and so unexpected that every lion in the cage started, and the next moment there was a scene of the wildest confusion.

The animals roared, jumped from their pedestals, and soon pinned the man to the floor. By a supreme effort he raised himself, and being near the door, the attendants were able to keep the lions back by firing blank cartridges until he could get out. But he was terribly mauled, and it was a long and tedious illness which followed. To show what a disturbing effect that shout had on the lions, it was hours before they could be quieted, and even when they were fed, two hours afterward, they were still restless and excited, and left their meat every few minutes to roar and growl.

That was the last time the trainer ever entered the cage. He lost his nerve completely. Unless a man has absolute self-control, he can never be sure of what may happen to him as a lion-trainer. This trainer's sudden loss of patience proved that he was unable to control his feelings, in itself a weakness, and animals recognize all weaknesses immediately.

Among other things, physical agility is a prime requisite. It is better if it is the agility of reserve rather than the agility of aggres-

CAPTAIN JACK BONAVITA

sion, for aggression arouses a like quality in the animal, and develops an appreciation of his brute strength, which sooner or later may be used against the trainer. But the equipoise and power existing only in those of good personal habits and judgment give an animal trainer the needed ability to escape an otherwise unavoidable danger.

Another quality is nerve—and plenty of it. Without nerve no man can do anything with a wild animal; it is the secret of the animal trainer's success, while ceaseless vigilance means the safety of his life. A man may be nervous and yet have plenty of nerve. I have known trainers who would start at the slightest noise or a sudden sound, and who would rather walk ten miles out of their way than meet a stranger, or attract attention in any way; and yet in times of danger, when their lives hung in the balance, would exhibit the utmost nerve and daring, mixed with a calm assurance that was astonishing.

These personal qualities are more or less apparent to all close observers of animal training, but there is one which is even more essential than any of the others, and for which the trainer seldom gets credit, yet it is one which places his profession on a par with that of the school-teacher, the preacher, the writer, or any of the students of men, because the study is more difficult and more complex.

This is a knowledge of animal nature, as diversified and peculiar, and as subject to varying conditions and environment, as human nature. Some may say that it is not as complex as human nature, because it is not as highly organized, but it furnishes the same food for thought, with the added element that upon the trainer's knowledge of the idiosyncrasies of his charges depends his success, and very often his life.

Constant vigilance, not only in the arena, but out of it, is the trainer's watchword. Consequently, trainers are a hard-working lot; for it is not only the actual public performances which take up their time. It is necessary to have constant rehearsals, constant lessons to the animals about various things; for it is never wise to try to correct or teach much during a performance, and there is always much to learn and study. Many animals drop off in time, either by sickness or from some other causes, and new animals have to be trained to take their place: this is always done privately, and few ever realize the amount of time and trouble that an animal will sometimes require before he is perfected in one little act.

The ideal animal trainer is a man of superb physique. His eyes are clear, his muscles hard and sinewy, his limbs well grown, his body well developed, and his clean, healthy skin shows the warm blood circulating beneath. He is without blemish physically, and his mental capabilities are good. He knows men as well as animals. He makes a versatile application of that knowledge; he knows the traits, the history, and the tendencies of those animals which form his life study, and on the constant use of that knowledge depends his dominance.

I have always been particularly fortunate in my trainers. From the time when I assumed control of the business in 1881, it has been my good fortune to have intelligent men, who take an interest in and love their profession, and who love their animals and charges.

Edward Deyerling, chief animal trainer at the Chicago Exposition in 1893, received his tuition under me in England in the eighties.

His persistency in practice was remarkable, and while his methods with his animals gained their entire confidence in him, the unearthly hours which he devoted to their education would have told on the vitality of many men of stronger constitution than his. The success he attained was more than well deserved. He was a humane trainer and possessed those good qualities so essential for success in the art of animal subjugation.

He was not killed, as is generally believed, but died a natural death several years ago.

The wild animal performances of 1893 were small affairs compared with the exhibitions of to-day, but his performance with five male lions gave the World's Fair visitors much to talk about, and secured for him a great reputation in this country, and I am naturally proud that he began his career in one of my establishments.

But I am prouder still of a lion-trainer who is with me now, Captain Jack Bonavita, who has trained no less than twenty-seven grown lions to perform in the arena at the same time. That this has been the work of years it is hardly necessary to state; but the patience, courage, judgment, and terrible nerve-strain necessary to reach this climax no one can ever realize except those who have watched him carefully week after week, month after month, and year after year.

There were times when it seemed as though he would certainly have to abandon his task; there was so much to contend with, so many difficulties to face and overcome, and such bitter disappointments. But Bonavita is a man of iron will, and when once he has made up his mind to do a thing, he never rests until he has accomplished it thoroughly.

When he first made his appearance at the Pan-American Exhibition in 1901, his entrance with the twenty-seven lions was so impressive that for a few seconds after the first flare of the band the silence was intense. Few will forget that incident. The gates at the back of the arena opened, and slowly and majestically out walked twenty-seven kings of the forest, and at the unspoken order of one man,—for he never speaks to them when performing,—each one took his special place on a certain pedestal, and went through all the various evolutions and acts in which he had been so carefully trained. The sight of this one man moving quietly about among all the lions made a deep impression upon many people.

President Roosevelt remarked, after witnessing his performance, that he had never seen or heard of anything like it, and that he admired the man's pluck, for he was a hero. General Miles wrote from the War Office, and said:

" I was particularly impressed with Bonavita and his monster grouping of twenty-seven lions. Such control of these noble creatures as was shown is truly remarkable."

The first impression one gets of Captain Bonavita is that of a refined and courteous gentleman. He is peculiarly reserved, and it is with the greatest reluctance that he can ever be induced to talk about himself, but he is never tired of talking about his lions.

He is of an extremely sensitive, highly strung nature, and although many feel that his nerves must be of steel, there are times when the terrible strain is more than unusually severe, and he retires to his own quarters completely played out. For it is absurd to think that a man who does such a risky thing as he does is never nervous. He realizes his danger as much as any one, and he has had cause to do so many times.

His chief comforts seem to be his cat and dog. The dog, a magnificent Great Dane named Pluto, is devoted to his master, and after a specially trying time, when he seems quite unable to speak to any one else, the master talks to him. The cat, named Tramp, has no pedigree whatever, and is as commonplace-looking an animal as can be found in any back yard. But Captain Bonavita is almost as devoted to him as to the dog, and when the cat sits on the dog's back the man who can control twenty-seven lions is perfectly satisfied.

I have spoken of some of his accidents in

other chapters. In all Captain Bonavita has had over fifty bad ones, but these have not prevented his going among the lions again at the very first opportunity. To use his own words: "A man does not refuse to go into battle because he has been hurt."

Another trainer who has become famous through her daring and wonderful control of the most treacherous of wild beasts is Mme. Louise Morelli. She is a Frenchwoman, and talks to her jaguars, leopards, and panthers in French, which they appear to understand quite as well as any other language, as it is not so much what is said as the tone of voice in which the words are spoken.

Mme. Morelli is a small woman and rather frail, but her nerve and quiet self-possession are truly wonderful. Leopards, panthers, and jaguars are noted for their stealthy, sly ways, and their deceit and treachery. They are most difficult to train and subdue, and can never be relied upon. These cringing big cats are the most alert fiends by nature; they have none of the nobility of the lion, none of the aloofness of the tiger. They are cowardly

MADAME MORELLI AND HER JAGUARS, PANTHERS,
AND LEOPARDS

and sly, and are always watching an opportunity to spring on the trainer's back on the slightest provocation, so that the training of them is more perilous than work with any other animals. And yet this small woman goes into the arena with five of them, makes them go through various acts and manœuvers, and finally sits down among them and allows one or two of them to lick her hands, and even to take them in their treacherous mouths.

This is dangerous enough, but the most dangerous trick of all is when she allows one of her jaguars, Cartouche, to place the weight of his prostrate body on a stick held horizontally in her hands and over her face, while she looks up into his glaring eyes.

Herman Weedon is noted for his mixed groups, of which I have already spoken. He has unlimited courage and daring, and is a splendid trainer, but runs a terrible risk in dealing with Goldie, who is one of the fiercest and most dangerous tigresses. Time after time he has been terribly torn and lacerated by this animal, and time after time he has been warned to give up all attempts at training her and leave her out of the group altogether. But one might as well ask a mountain to move as to ask Weedon to give up Goldie. In spite of her treachery and vindictiveness, he is truly fond of her. He will take the trouble to explain over and over again that it is only occasionally that she has these wicked fits, that often she is most gentle and affectionate, and that she has such a beautiful head and body that it would completely spoil his group to leave her out.

And although all he has ever been able to make her do is to sit on a pedestal and ladder and allow him to open her mouth, he persists in trying, with wonderful and unlimited patience, to subdue that terrible, passionate nature of hers, and induce her to be a little more tractable. He is afraid of nothing, and trouble and opposition only make him more determined to overcome obstacles and attain his object.

A wonderful proof of training is the man-ape, or chimpanzee, Consul. This animal eats and drinks like a human being, plays the piano, uses a typewriter, and behaves in such a won-

derfully human way that one begins to wonder whether Darwin's theory is not right,
after all.

Charles Day is one of the oldest trainers in
the exhibition, and has been in the Bostock
family for thirty years. The fascination of
this life is well shown in his case. At one
time he was also a trainer of lions, but now
contents himself with showing visitors round
and explaining the various zoölogical specimens. He has had more unique experiences
than any man I know, and tells them in a very
dramatic and amusing manner.

CHAPTER XIII

ACCIDENTS

EVERY man or woman who trains animals has what are termed "accidents."
Animals differ in temperament, mood, and nature as human beings do, and the trainer
learns to read the intent of each in his eye,
in the motions of his tail, in his walk and
movement.

Animals are erratic and uncertain at times,
and one can never tell just what the animal
will do. He may have done the same things
a great number of times easily and willingly,
and yet may, without any warning, suddenly
refuse to do anything further. He comes out
with a plain, blunt refusal, without any apolo-
gies, either in voice or manner, and he usually
makes it pretty clear that he means what he
says. He has grown rebellious; his sense

of wrongs, his hate, and his desire for revenge appear to have culminated suddenly, and his only wish is to get even with those who have been making him do things which made him look ridiculous.

In a case like this there is generally an accident, and if the trainer is not alert and self-possessed he is apt to lose his life. Again, an animal may lose his temper suddenly, and in one of those swift rages or frenzies into which all wild animals are liable to fall at any time try to kill his trainer, and a few moments afterward crawl back and show his repentance. It is most unwise to punish an animal when this happens. He will probably do the same thing again, and may succeed in killing his trainer the next time, but to punish him when he is repentant would only make him vindictive and revengeful, and wild animals do not forget easily.

Of course, no animal is ever to be trusted until he is dead; but if the trainer is in a cage and gets cornered, experience teaches him what to do. He learns to think and act quickly, to retain a natural sobriety and coolness, never to lose his temper with a wild beast, and to make him obey every time, at all costs. It is never the physical force of the trainer that conquers; that is impossible. It is his coolness, determination, and untiring patience.

More minor injuries are received in training, without any evil intent on the part of the animal, than in any other way. The lion, for instance, is always clumsy, and is at any time likely to misplace a paw armed with claws that could not be more effective if they were fashioned from so much steel. If that paw passes along the body of the trainer, the unlucky man goes to the hospital, where he may be laid up for six or seven weeks.

Such an accident happened to Mme. Pianka one night at Buffalo. An admirer had sent her a bouquet of red roses, and in place of her heavy riding-whip she carried it into the arena for her performance with the lions. It is a fallacy to suppose that any change in the dress of the trainer will make a difference with the animal. All trained animals know their trainers, and even should another man come in dressed in the same clothes as their own trainer, they would recognize the difference instantly. But all animals will jump for meat, no matter where that meat may be.

There can be no doubt whatever that in this instance the lions at the first glance mistook the bunch of red roses for red meat. One lion had not yet reached his pedestal when Mme. Pianka entered, or possibly he might not have sprung. But, being on the floor of the arena, the moment he caught sight of the red mass in her hand he sprang forward, and in the wide sweep of his paw to get the supposed meat, struck the trainer's cheek, and the blow, glancing to her arm and chest, tore her flesh and dress.

Instantly Mme. Pianka tossed the flowers from her, and she was only just in time, for every one of the lions pounced upon them, sniffed and smelled them with evident surprise and disgust, found they were not what they had expected, and in their usual slow, deliberate manner remounted their pedestals and waited passively for their act. Mme. Pianka, who is an extremely plucky woman and possesses great nerve and self-possession, put them through their usual performance, although her face, neck, and arms were bleeding profusely, and then, as she left the arena, fainted.

Again, what begins by accident may be quickly turned to murderous account by the animals. The most perilous thing a man can do is to lose his footing, for it is more than likely, the moment he falls, the animal will spring upon him. An English trainer was almost torn to pieces once because of a pair of heavy top-boots he wore.

One of his tigers slipped, and in trying to save himself got one of his claws entangled in the trainer's leg. It was a purely accidental blow, and the tiger, alarmed, tried to get away, but the keen claws had penetrated through the stiff leather, and in endeavoring to extricate them the animal threw his master down. Quick as a flash the two other tigers in the cage were on the prostrate trainer, and but for the prompt action of an assistant who pluckily sprang into the cage and beat them back, the trainer would never have come out

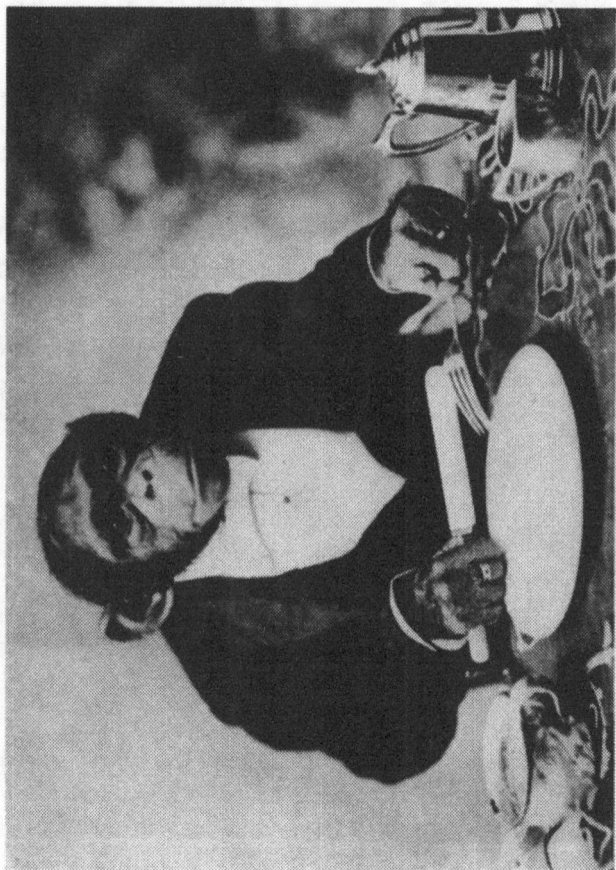

"CONSUL," THE CHIMPANZEE

alive. It is a vital article in the code of every trainer never to lose his temper in a case of this kind or to punish the innocent cause of it. Often the animals themselves are as much frightened as the trainer, and their only resource when frightened is to fight, and to fight with all their inherent fierceness and strength.

Therefore, to punish an animal for what is perfectly natural to him would not only be the height of absurdity, but most unwise and dangerous. Wild animals can never be punished by chastisement; a few harsh words are generally sufficient, and even then there is the danger that it may be too much. Anger the animal or irritate him, and he is likely to seek revenge with a prompt spring or a sweeping blow.

The apparent lashes given with the whip during performances are mere pretenses, part of the daily program, and known to the animals as such. True, these supposed lashings call forth growls and snarls, but this is because the animal knows it is a signal for him to do something, and he does not often feel

12

inclined to do it. He generally does it, but he always protests a little if he can, and growls and snarls form his speech.

Expert, indeed, must be the trainer, for if one of these light blows should go wrong and land on some part of the animal's body where it would hurt, there might well be an attack; almost certainly there would be a fit of sulks on the part of the animal struck while doing his best that would not only put an end to any further effort on his part for that day, but even mean lifelong resentment and hatred, which would simply wait for a favorable opportunity for injuring the trainer who had given the blow.

To illustrate this. A trainer was one day exercising his animals, and in using the whip accidentally caught a lion on the tip of his nose. For a moment the animal paused, as though too surprised to do anything else; then he rubbed his nose reflectively, as though still trying to solve the problem. The trainer, who had at first grown rigid with fear of what might follow, kept a careful eye on the lion; but as he appeared quiet and only puzzled, and as the trainer concluded the blow could have hurt him only slightly, he thought that was the end of it.

The animals were driven back to their cages, and nothing happened to show that the injured lion remembered it in any way. But that same evening, when the time came for the performance, and the trainer flicked his whip toward the lion whom he had accidentally struck, the animal, instead of taking it as his cue, promptly roused himself, gathered himself together, and in another moment had sprung full at the trainer.

Fortunately, the trainer had noticed the dangerous symptoms,—for a lion generally gives a little warning before he springs, a tiger never,—and had leaped aside with such agility that the lion landed a little to the right, and this time received a stinging blow which sent him back for a moment, giving the trainer just time to escape.

But from that time it was found absolutely impossible to make that lion perform. He would go into the arena, and would even mount his pedestal, but at the very first flick or lash of the whip in his direction he would prepare to spring. Therefore, through a very slight accident,—a little blow which one would think such a big brute would not mind,—we lost one of our best performers.

Some very serious accidents have also occurred from the playfulness of animals. A playful animal is always dangerous; he may be in the best of moods and tempers, and simply wish to have a romp, but his strength and power are too overwhelming for a man to have anything to do with him. The wisest course to pursue with an animal in a playful mood is to get out of his way and leave him alone.

This is easy enough at rehearsal, but in the performance it is another matter. The animal must be put through his paces day after day, or he will expect to take it easy all the time. A good trainer will always try, when possible, to let the animal have his play out before urging him to perform; but sometimes this play will go on until the audience becomes impatient, and then comes the risk to the trainer. The animal is comfortable and enjoying him-

CAPTAIN BONAVITA CARRYING A LION WEIGHING FIVE HUNDRED POUNDS

self, and to be forced to get up on a pedestal
and do other things in the middle of it must
naturally be irritating and annoying, and the
animal generally vents this annoyance and ir-
ritability on the one who forces him to act.
In some cases he will not be forced, and then
more trouble still arises for the trainer.

I was once working with a group of lions
at Indianapolis, when an incident occurred
which will show how one small playful action
on the part of a wild animal may sometimes
lead to serious results. I was in the training-
school when Young Wallace, one of my
fiercest lions, but for whom I had a great affection, which, in a way, he appeared to return, jumped from his pedestal for a piece of
meat which I had thrown on the floor. While
eating the meat, I stood watching him, and
thoughtlessly tapping the leather leg of my
training-boot with my whip.

Wallace had been accustomed to playing
with the whip, and to feel the gentle stroking
of it down the muscles of his back. One of
the tricks which he had been taught was to
ask for the stroking by reaching for the whip

18

with his paw when it was held suspended over him. A lion's paw is no plaything. A cat's paw, with its sharp, incisive claws hidden in the velvet, is sometimes a fierce and effective weapon. Imagine a cat's paw enlarged twenty times, propelled with a proportionate increase of muscular energy, and with the same lightning-like rapidity, and you can gather some little idea of what a lion's paw means when it strikes.

In this instance, Wallace struck at me merely in play and with little of the strength that he would have displayed in a wilful attack. The stroke was a part of the trick he was used to, and he made it with good animal intention, but it was none the less direful. The claws fastened deep into the fleshy part of my leg, through boot and underclothing, and there stuck. A lion's claws would not be nearly so dangerous were they sharp and straight; but they have a sharp curve, and go in like a cant-hook, penetrating the flesh at an acute angle. The lion has not the sense to draw them out, as they went in, by the curving process, but pulls them straight out.

Wallace found his claws in farther than he intended, and, slightly frightened, promptly drew them out, not backward but forward. Needless to say, with them came a good-sized piece of flesh, which caused me excruciating pain.

Painful as it was, I did not move, knowing as I did that to show any signs of fear or trepidation would cause alarm, and, probably, not only be the spoiling of the lion, but the signal for an attack. But when a second or two had elapsed, and Wallace had returned to eating his meat, I at once ordered the animals back to their cages, and in this way Wallace, picking up the remains of his meat and taking them with him, was soon in his cage again, without having been given time or opportunity to realize that he had hurt his trainer or drawn blood—two things which always have bad effects on animals.

A great many accidents occur, and always will occur, either through carelessness or through mistakes on the part of those in attendance on the animals. It is not only the trainers who suffer from the claws and teeth

of the animals: there are numerous other men
and boys in an exhibition who are constantly
running into danger, very often when there is
not the slightest occasion for their doing so.

The duties of these attendants are numerous. Besides helping to keep the animals and
cages clean, they have to attend to watering
the animals, see that no bones or other small
articles are in the cages,—for the smallest object, no matter how worthless, may be the
means of leading two animals to quarrel for
its possession,—and do a hundred and
one other things which crop up from day to
day.

Many of these attendants also help the
trainers, which is almost as dangerous as the
duties of the trainer himself. Properties and
other things have to be passed in to the trainer
during the rehearsals and performances,
doors and gates have to be opened and fastened after them, and there is always the possibility that an animal may turn and spring
on the attendant, although with trained animals this rarely happens. It is nothing for a
man to close a door, but if an animal springs

back at it, it would require more than the
strength of six to do so.

An attendant was holding the door open, after a performance, for some bears to return to
their cages. All but one bear—a big Kadiak
—had gone quietly in, when, without the least
warning, the bear turned, inserted his claws
round the edge of the door, tearing it out of
the hands of the attendant, and in a second
had him down. In spite of the promptest assistance given by Mr. Stevenson, who risked
his life in so doing, the man's arm was terribly torn, and it was months before he was
able to leave the hospital. To this day his arm
has remained stiff, and he can only hold it in
an unnatural way.

A terrible accident took place entirely
through a mistake on the part of an employee.
Albert Neilson by name and a good, hard-
working young fellow, and a great favorite
with the show, nicknamed " Curly," was sent
one morning with some food in a basket to
feed some young lion cubs. The cubs were in
a cage next to Rajah, the big tiger. All the
employees had been repeatedly warned about

taking care in going anywhere near this tiger
—a special little trick of his being to feign
sleep and then suddenly throw out a paw with
claws extended.

Whether "Curly" was careless and mistook the cage will never be known, but the
other attendants were appalled by terrible
screams issuing from Rajah's cage, and on
rushing forward saw to their horror that the
man was being held in the tiger's mouth by
his head. The details are too terrible to go
into, but here again Mr. Stevenson, who
has earned for himself the name of the
Guardian Angel of the Show, rushed into
the cage, and, at the peril of his life, did his
best with iron bars to force the tiger to let go.

But nothing would induce the beast to re-
lax his hold, and in the midst of his growling
the man was calling piteously for help. After
this, pistols were fired at him; but, when
warned to come out, Sam Stevenson would
not leave the man, although he was surrounded by bullets, each one of which was
likely to strike him at any moment. Rajah
was hit once or twice, but he only let go his

hold on the man's head to take a firmer one round his waist.

Neilson was eventually drawn out, but he died soon afterward, to the deep grief of all in the show. Most trainers are superstitious, and great attention was drawn at the time to the fact of the number thirteen playing so prominent a part in the boy's history. He was born on the thirteenth, had thirteen letters in his name, and so forth.

It is, perhaps, the living in this perpetual state or atmosphere of danger which causes indifference and, in some cases, neglect on the part of the attendants. Each man and boy knows perfectly well that he is daily exposed to bites and scratches, and, perhaps, fearful mutilation; for all this is carefully impressed on every newcomer,—sometimes so much so that they depart with a shiver, which proves them totally unsuitable. The treachery of the animals is almost daily demonstrated in some way or another; the attendants are often witnesses of what terrible things wild animals can do, and yet I have seen them pass close to the cages, or stand indifferently by them, when every moment they were risking the loss of a limb, and, perhaps, their lives.

I am always afraid of accidents with an extremely quiet man,—a man, that is, who never speaks to or appears to take any notice of the animals. All wild animals are very sensitive, and seem to know instinctively when people are interested in them. A friendly word or a little interest goes a long way with them. Captain Bonavita, for instance, never speaks to his lions when performing, but he loves his animals and takes the greatest interest in them, and when in their cages talks to each one by name.

Whenever I notice an attendant who evidently takes no interest whatever in the animals, I invariably get rid of him. He may be in the show for some time, but one of these days the animals will get him; so, to prevent a bad "accident," I consider it wise to let him go.

A very small error is often the cause of a serious accident, and this I experienced myself at one time with Rajah, the tiger who killed Albert Neilson. I had been putting this

MR. SAM STEVENSON

*Whose bravery in saving lives has earned
for him the sobriquet of "The
Guardian Angel"*

animal through his rehearsal one day, and was returning through the runway to shut him in his cage. By an error on the part of an attendant, the door was not shut as it should have been, and Rajah had an opportunity to jump on my defenseless back. It was an opportunity he did not hesitate to seize immediately. The indiscretion of this attendant nearly cost me my life. Rajah got his fangs inside the head-protector I wore, and his claws into my body. After the first terrible sensation of tearing, I remember nothing more, for I became unconscious, and, in addition to other injuries, had concussion of the brain afterward.

A similar accident happened to Captain Bonavita. He was putting his lions back, when one door, which had not been properly fastened, was pushed open by one of the lions, who sprang upon the trainer and nearly killed him. Another time, when Bonavita was in the runway behind the cages exercising his lions, the electric lights suddenly went out. This was a fearful predicament. Owing to the hubbub which immediately ensued in the building, it was impossible to make any one hear, and even had he done so, it would have taken a very brave man to go into a dark runway with several lions.

As it was, Captain Bonavita did the best he could. He kept swinging about him the heavy club he had in his hand. He could hear one of the lions coming toward him in the dark and breathing heavily. He knew only too well that the momentary pause was the signal either for creeping nearer to him or for a spring. As long as he was able to keep the club swinging he knew the lion was at a certain distance, but in an instant it came in contact with something soft, and as this was followed by a fierce growl, the trainer knew he had probably struck the lion on the nose just as he was creeping close up to him.

His arms were beginning to ache terribly, and he realized that he would be unable to keep it up much longer, but when he struck the soft substance a second time, and knew that the lion had again crept closer, he determined to sell his life dearly, and kept up the swinging movements, although he was beginning to get faint and dizzy from the exertion. As long as he could keep this going he was comparatively safe, but there was always the danger that, instead of creeping nearer, the lion might spring, and in that case nothing could save him.

Just as he was about to give up and take the consequences, the lights suddenly came on again, and disclosed the lion in the very act of preparing for a spring. The sudden glare of the light, however, and the appearance of the trainer standing there with his club, appeared to confuse him; and when Bonavita, with a supreme effort, ordered him back, he turned round and went submissively into his cage. The trainer walked to the end of the runway, where he was found by the attendants soon afterward in a state of collapse from exhaustion.

It takes so little to turn a trivial incident into a serious matter, that the greatest care is always necessary. In moving round the arena at one performance, Mme. Morelli in some way touched one of the leopards with the lace of her dress. This was before they

had all mounted to their pedestals. The lace
of the dress caught him in the eye, and in an
instant the leopard sprang, and had she not
been so fortunate as to catch him with her
whip as she sprang aside, there would probably have been a very serious accident. The
spring of a leopard is a serious thing; it can
bound ten or twelve feet in the air, and although it is the lightest and most graceful
jumper of all the wild animals, it is also the
strongest, and it was only the agility and
prompt action of Mme. Morelli which saved
her.

At another time, a slight oversight on
Mme. Morelli's part resulted in a very serious accident. She had concluded her performance, and was leaving the arena, thinking all the leopards were in front of her, when
an attendant called out that one leopard was
staying behind and creeping toward her.
Quick as the attendant had been in warning
her, and quick as Mme. Morelli was, they
were neither of them quick enough that time;
for before she could turn round, the leopard
sprang, and, unfortunately, catching her just

POLAR BEARS AT PLAY

as she was in the act of turning, landed on her neck and shoulders, tearing them fearfully.

In this instance it was Captain Bonavita who rushed in and saved her, beating the leopard back and keeping it at bay until Mme. Morelli was safely out of the way, and the animal could be sent back to its cage. This was one of the most serious accidents she ever had, and great persuasion was brought to bear on her afterward to give up that leopard, but she would not hear of it. She was ill for some time, but as soon as she was able she re-entered the arena and made each leopard obey her as before. It is always a matter of wonder to see leopards perform, but to see four or five do so with one small woman is a marvelous sight, and proves what can be done in the way of mastering even such treacherous and vindictive creatures as leopards and jaguars.

In taking up the business of an animal trainer, a man, if he has the qualities of which I have already spoken, runs no more desperate chances than thousands of other men who follow their various callings. The physician risks his life daily from infectious diseases, but beyond taking a few precautions, such a thing as thinking of the danger never occurs to him. The soldier knows he may be called to give up his life for his country in time of war, but when face to face with the enemy, he only nerves himself to think of his duty, and not of the danger to himself.

There are hundreds of occupations, such as mining, building, tunneling, and driving railway engines, where men also run daily risks, and an animal trainer runs no more than any of these, provided he is careful and cautious. Animal trainers are no different from other men. They all have the same capacity for fear that every man has in time of great danger, but they have schooled themselves, by good habits and self-control, to meet the danger calmly.